STEVEN

REAPER'S LAMENT

AVIATION STORIES BY PILOTS WHO
SHOULD BE DEAD

outskirts
press

Books by Steven Lane Smith

Reaper's Lament
Alibi for a Vigilante
Caledonia Switch
A Dolphin and a Pilot
Fair Share
Salvation at Rio Feo

stevenlanesmith.com

For Gray and Miriam

CONTENTS

Image credit: Nomadsoul1/depositphotos.com

THE GRIM REAPER

CHAPTER 1

GRIM REAPER

CALL ME WHAT you will -- Angel of Death, Prince of Doom, Grim Reaper. A scourge of humanity, I inflict on humans pestilence, fire, and war. I've brandished my scythe for centuries, and I've exterminated humans by the millions. I collect them singly, too, in the dark of night or in the glittering light of day.

How I love to harvest the aviators, those brash souls who fight me every inch of the way! I take them as best I can when their caution lapses or when they dare to fly farther, higher, faster. I blind them with snow and lashing rain. I weigh them down with ice, break them apart with violent shears of wind, and exhaust their fuel. I smash them together, spin them into space, and cast them against the ground.

Although it grieves me mightily to admit it, some of them have escaped my blade.

Here are their stories.

Tracy W. Price

Centerville, Ohio
Wright State University
Captain, Southwest Airlines
Twin Cessnas, Piper & Beechcraft
Turboprops, *Citation* 550,
YS-11, DHC-8, BAe-146,
B-737-200, -300, -500, -700, -800, -Max 8
Airborne Express, Presidential Airways,
Southwest Airlines

CHAPTER 2

ICE

ALTHOUGH THE COCKPIT was as cold as an igloo, I had good reason to perspire as if I were in a sauna. In the middle of a night darker than a grizzly bear's armpit, I was alone in a Cessna 404 cruising at 160 knots through fog, drizzle, and heavy clouds in forecast icing conditions. My aircraft had been loaded to its maximum gross weight. Not long after I had departed from Spartanburg, South Carolina on my way to Toledo, Ohio, I was no longer in radar contact, so I couldn't request radar controller vectors away from the trouble that lay ahead.

Ice began to accumulate on my aircraft. Soon, three inches of a nasty mix of clear and rime ice covered the fuselage and wings. I activated inflatable rubber bladders called "boots" (designed to shed ice from the leading edges of the wings and tail). The de-ice boots inflated and deflated furiously, but they were fighting a losing battle. I turned on propeller heat, and ice started breaking off the propellers and slamming against the fuselage like shots from a cannon.

The cockpit windows were almost completely covered with ice. My plane was rapidly becoming the world's largest ice sculpture. Weight and drag were increasing and lift was decreasing, exactly the opposite trends any pilot would want to see. My airspeed was deteriorating even though I pushed the propeller controls full forward and the throttles to

3

maximum. The turbochargers boosted the manifold pressure over the red line and the engines screamed a high-pitched yowl, but I couldn't maintain airspeed in level flight. The engine cylinder head temperatures flirted with their yellow arcs. I didn't know how long the finicky engine gear boxes could stand the strain. Both engines wailing at maximum power couldn't keep the airspeed from falling off steadily. At 90 knots, the airplane shuddered violently and the right wing dropped forty-five degrees. I had stalled. I recovered, but buffeting warned me of an imminent second stall. I lowered the nose as required to maintain 95 knots. The airplane was in an 800-feet-per-minute descent toward mountainous terrain.

The unforgiving 6,684-foot peak of Mount Mitchell, North Carolina was obscured by darkness and clouds somewhere just outside my cockpit as ice dragged me down below 6,600 feet. I was a twenty-year-old charter pilot with two thousand flight hours flying a block of ice on the edge of a stall waiting for a wall of granite to end it all. No wonder I was sweating. Eddie Rickenbacker would have been sweating, too.

Then a wonderful thing happened. The outside air temperature warmed to one degree above freezing. The clouds thinned out. The drizzle slacked. Ice began to loosen its grip. My engines were still screaming as the aircraft leveled off. The airspeed increased to 105 knots and I started a slow constant-speed climb. From barely one hundred feet per minute, the rate of climb increased to five hundred feet per minute. When I reached 7,000 feet, I pulled the throttles back to bring the manifold pressures below the red line. I managed to maintain a climb rate of 600 feet per minute at 115 knots. Passing through 7,500 feet, I asked a sleepy air traffic controller for the latest altimeter setting and requested 8,000 feet for a cruising altitude. By then I was east of

Johnson City, Tennessee, north of the highest of the Smokey Mountains and out of icing conditions.

The sky was filled with stars like diamonds on black velvet. My airspeed was stable at 160 knots. My engines were purring. I examined my beautiful, clean, perfectly-shaped wing. That moment was a high point of gratitude and humility in my life. I felt the purest form of elation I had ever known. I had never felt so alive!

Many years have passed. Even though I'm a senior airline captain now who's survived my share of adversity logging more than 28,000 flying hours, I've never forgotten the night back in 1981 when the Reaper loaded me up with ice, pushed me down into the mountains, and, then, thank God, let me go.

Jack Broughton

Lake Forest, California
United States Military Academy
National War College
Colonel, United States Air Force
Thunderbird Lead
P-47, P-51, F-80, F-84, F-86, F-100,
F-101, F-102, F-104, F-105, F-106
Antilles Airboats, Mobil,
Rockwell International

CHAPTER 3

TOBOGGAN

TO BREAK the Grim Reaper's cold heart, let him think he's got you in the bag and let him count you among the dead before he's actually squeezed the last breath out of you, and then, as he prematurely howls in victory, do the impossible to break free of his deadly grasp.

Three days after a young F-105 *Thunderchief* (*Thud*) pilot named Joe had been shot down over North Vietnam, Lieutenant Colonel Jack Broughton led *Wabash*, a flight of four F-105s, in an attempt to locate Joe so he could be rescued. North Vietnamese MiGs and surface-to-air missiles hampered *Wabash Flight's* efforts. Broughton had to keep his formation safe from hostile fire while switching from one garbled radio frequency to another to coordinate with other fighters, radar controllers, rescue elements, and in-flight refueling tankers. His time-remaining-on-station was dwindling as his fuel quantity gauge unwound toward zero.

He sent *Wabash Three* and *Four* to a tanker to take on enough fuel to return to replace him and his wingman Ken so they, too, could leave the search to refuel. He methodically overflew the ridge where Joe's parachute likely had landed. Broughton assumed that Joe was on the move to evade search parties of enemy soldiers. Broughton needed to establish Joe's precise location to justify another search effort the following morning, so he persisted in trying to establish radio contact. He radioed in the blind for Joe to turn on his emergency beacon. When the weak sound of an emergency beacon responded, Broughton radioed for Joe to turn off the high-pitched transmitter, and the squealing ceased. Broughton was elated.

As Broughton and Ken continued to search, their fuel gauges sank well below "bingo" -- a dangerously low state. Broughton received troubling news of a delayed rendezvous between *Wabash Three/Four* and their in-flight refueling tanker. The two planes still hadn't returned to continue the search when Broughton was forced to suspend the hunt and to head south to find a tanker.

Broughton climbed to altitude to conserve fuel. He urgently requested vectors toward the nearest tanker, but repeated radio calls failed to raise a radar controller. A tanker pilot overheard Broughton's plea for help, and he did his best to raise a controller, too. Nothing. Broughton and the tanker pilot tried to coordinate their own rendezvous, but neither Broughton nor his wingman had enough fuel remaining to reach the tanker. *Wabash One* and *Two* were minutes away from becoming gliders.

Because ejection from their fuel-starved *Thuds* seemed imminent, Broughton faced an unwelcome truth: natives in the region below them were known for skinning captured airmen alive! He and his wingman were floundering in deep water: he had only 700 pounds of fuel remaining; his wingman, only 500. Miraculously, before Broughton had to make reservations at the Hanoi Hilton, a confident voice came over the radio. It was the aircraft commander of *Tanker White*, who identified Broughton's radar return forty miles ahead. *Tanker White* told Broughton to start a turn to the east and to descend toward 24,000 feet so the tanker could close the distance across the arc of Broughton's left-hand turn.

"Two hundred pounds," Ken radioed. Two hundred pounds of fuel might last for four minutes, an exceedingly short time when flying over people who had reasons to hate American pilots and who were willing to show it by ripping off Ken's head and skinning him like a squirrel.

Tanker White gained on *Wabash One* and *Two*. Broughton's fuel tanks had 300 pounds of JP-4 remaining. He visually acquired the tanker closing from seven-to-eight o'clock behind him and radioed a simple message to Ken.

"Go get him."

Ken barrel rolled to flush the tanker out in front of him and to place his F-105 near the pre-contact position on the tanker's boom. As Ken approached the pre-contact position, his last drop of fuel was spent and the fire in his engine went out.

"I've flamed out," Ken radioed. "*Tanker White*, you've got to toboggan at two-fifty to give me a chance."

"Tobogganing at two-fifty" meant descending at a constant speed of 250 knots so Ken could glide to the contact position just aft of the boom. *Tanker White* started an immediate descent at 250 knots, and Ken glided into contact position, giving the boom operator one chance at plugging him. The boom operator skillfully thrust the nozzle into the refueling receptacle in the nose of Ken's *Thud*. The hydraulic locks of the receptacle clamped onto the nozzle and held on. Without a word being exchanged, fuel started flowing into Ken's fuel tanks. The sound of igniters clicked in his helmet ear phones just before his wind-milling engine restarted.

While maintaining formation on Ken's wing, Broughton scanned his fuel gauge. Empty. Ken finished taking on a thousand pounds of fuel before disconnecting from the boom and moving aside to make room for his leader, who slid smoothly into contact position. The expert boom operator plugged Broughton's refueling receptacle barely seconds before Broughton's engine also would have flamed out. Broughton took on a full internal load of JP-4 before disconnecting and moving aside for Ken to do the same.

After refueling *the F-105s*, *Tanker White* no longer had enough fuel to return to its base, so the tanker pilot discontinued the toboggan maneuver and diverted to Takhli Royal Thai Air Force Base, Broughton's home base. The tanker pilot's quick decision-making had saved two *Thud* pilots from ejecting over enemy territory. The tanker aircraft commander had been prepared to face the consequences of doling out more than his authorized quantity of fuel to save Broughton and Ken from the Grim Reaper. The *Thud* pilots owed their lives to the pilot and crew of *Tanker White*, and Broughton thanked them again as soon as he landed at Takhli.

The Reaper wasn't completely shut out. On the following day, Broughton again flew fighter cover for a search-and-rescue effort to find Joe. The effort failed to pick up visual or audio clues of Joe's whereabouts. On the next day, Ken revisited the area on the way home from his bombing mission and was briefly heartened to receive a positive beeper response. When he attempted to authenticate Joe's identity, however, an Asian voice replied on the radio. The search for Joe was over. The enemy had finally found him. The Grim Reaper had claimed a good man.

Broughton, Jack. *Thud Ridge*. Bantam, 1969.

Colonel Broughton is the author of three books: *Thud Ridge*, *Going Downtown*, and *Rupert Red Two*.

Roger Champagne

Point Barrow, Alaska
Cessna 207, DHC-6, B-727, B-737
Cape Smythe Air Service
Wien Air Alaska

CHAPTER 4

ALASKA

ALASKA WAS A MAGNET back in my twenties, before GPS and ADS-B. I was well aware that the Reaper prowled the skies over the Last Frontier, home to more pilots per capita than anywhere else on earth. In Alaska, a state thirteen times the size of England with only one per cent of the population, an airplane crashed every other day and a pilot died about every ten days. Only a fifth of the state's 400 runways were paved. Jagged mountains jutted into the sky and weather often changed violently. As a new pilot hungry for experience, I had to go north, north to Alaska.

Airplanes were synonymous with travel in Alaska. People commuted to work and to school by plane. High school sports teams had no choice but to fly to away games because their only alternatives were unacceptably long journeys by snow machine or dog sled. Many villages had no roads leading out of town. Cessna 207 *Caravans* and DHC-6 *Twin Otters* flown by air taxi operators were the backbones of Alaskan travel. If a guy in Napaskiak ordered a pizza, an airplane from Bethel would make the six-mile delivery because there was no bridge across the Kuskokwim River. That doesn't happen in the Lower Forty-Eight where conveniences like highways, bridges, and Uber cars are taken for granted.

I quickly adapted to the Alaskan way of doing things. I learned that IFRR meant, "I Follow Rivers and Roads." Pilots who flew in marginal conditions using ground features for navigation were called "scud runners." It wasn't unusual for a scud runner to fly in whiteout conditions beneath a 400-foot cloud deck following a river to reach a destination. Too often, the destination was a cemetery. I adapted to Alaskan ways, but I promised myself that I'd fly safely and live long enough to get an airline job. Along the way, the Reaper tested my resolve and came after me a couple of times.

I was scheduled to fly a Cessna 207 *Caravan* with Randy Crosby to pick up two passengers at Anaktuvuk Pass up in North Slope Borough. (Boroughs in Alaska are like counties in the Lower Forty-Eight.) Anaktuvuk Pass, population 300, was surrounded by mountains on the northern slope of the Brooks Range. It was the only Nunamiut Iñupiat (Eskimo) village left in Alaska.

Randy was a big man. He was so big that everyone called him "Sasquatch," but, because he was the chief pilot, they only called him Sasquatch when he wasn't around. He's not around now, so Sasquatch it is.

Summer days in North Slope Borough north of the 68th parallel were almost perpetual daylight. With plenty of sunshine to light the way and being ahead of schedule, there was no reason to hurry. You could say Sasquatch and I had idle hands, and we all know whose workshop you get with idle hands. I blame it all on Sasquatch. He was the old hand, a man of experience and influence. I was just a new guy along for the ride.

"What a beautiful place for a picnic," Sasquatch said as he banked and yawed the plane into a slip so he could admire a picturesque river.

He normally didn't talk much, so this was like the Gettysburg Address. He lined up on a sandy beach beside the river. We didn't have balloon tires installed on the *Caravan*, so I thought he intended to touch down on the sand long enough to test for firmness. Sasquatch had other ideas. He dropped some flaps and announced that he was going to land on a bar of sand that I honestly considered a tad on the short side. I also was surprised, because, even though I had seen many beautiful picnic spots in my life, I'd never felt the urge to land on any of them.

"How about the passengers up at the Pass?" I asked.

"We've got plenty of time," he replied.

I questioned how much time we had remaining on earth. Sasquatch braked hard to stop the *Caravan* in time. Sand can be hard or soft. This sand was soft, and, as he turned to taxi downwind, the nose wheel augured into the sand. The propeller blades sent rocks flying like ice cubes in a blender until he shut down the engine.

When the engine came to rest, I could see that the tips of the propellers were bent to the shape of plastic coffee spoons. I made a note to get some resumes and applications for new employment into circulation as soon as I got back to Point Barrow. First things first: there was no guarantee that either of us would ever get out of this remote, isolated, God-forsaken spit of sand beside one of Alaska's gazillion rivers. Sasquatch, who didn't appear to be completely sure of his own employment at the moment, asked a question.

"The props don't look too bad, do they?"

"No," I lied. I was thinking, *Compared to what*?

Sasquatch was an idea-generation machine. His first idea was to use planks from an abandon cabin across the river to make a ramp for pushing the plane out of the soft sand. I thought this was an ingenious solution until he told me to take off my pants.

"Why would I take off my pants?" I needed to know, because I had never been naked in the presence of a man on the edge of civilization before.

"So you won't die of hypothermia when you cross the river to get the planks."

He was the captain, the chief pilot, no less, so I took off my pants and started wading. The powerful current was the only thing preventing the water from freezing solid. Only up to mid-thigh, I had no feeling in my feet, my ankles, my shins, my knees, and other nearby regions. I spun around and retreated from the water to dry land.

"What are you doing?" Sasquatch asked.

"Avoiding hypothermia."

"Weak dick." He took off his shoes and pants and waded into the world's coldest river. I wasn't completely at ease standing on the beach, naked from the waist down, watching my chief pilot, also naked from the waist down, thrashing around and cursing the temperature and the current. He was back on shore faster than a rubber ball could bounce off a wall. "We'd never make it," he said.

I pulled my pants over my numb legs and donned my boots. My mind turned to matters of survival.

"Should we start a fire?"

"We'll be out of here in no time." The chief pilot was an optimist. Maybe that's why he was the chief pilot.

My brain began to work in overdrive. Using river rocks, I built a replica of Caesar's famous Appian Way as a ramp for the nose wheel of the *Caravan*. I tore apart cardboard boxes from the cargo compartment and lay the flattened corrugated sheets on top of the rocks. Sasquatch and I leaned the full weight of our bodies onto the aircraft tail to free the prop from the sand and to pivot the nose wheel onto the Appian Way. Sasquatch hopped into the cockpit to crank the motor. He added power while I pushed on a wing strut harder than I had ever pushed on anything in my life.

When we finally freed the plane from the sand, Sasquatch taxied into a kind of takeoff position and tested the engine at higher RPMs to find out how much manifold pressure he could get without shaking the plane to pieces. Fortunately, the damage to the prop was symmetrical. The vibration wasn't a fraction of what I had feared.

Sasquatch made it clear that his overriding priority was to protect his job as chief pilot by ensuring that the owner should never learn of our mishap. I concentrated on more fundamental issues such as whether the strip of sandy beach was long enough for takeoff. I gallantly volunteered to stay on the beach, reducing the gross weight of the *Caravan* and improving Sasquatch's chances of getting airborne (while decreasing my chances of being engulfed in a fireball if the takeoff didn't work out).

My suggestion hinted at cowardice, but, if Sasquatch were to crash on takeoff, I might never be found. Perhaps I could survive the night by starting a campfire with debris from the pending crash. Sasquatch didn't think much of my proposal, so I dreamed up another plan. It was a plan I called the "Boulder Plan." It was the plan we actually employed. I was flattered that the chief pilot chose my plan from all possible alternatives until I realized that there weren't that many possible alternatives.

We had to take off without digging a trench with the nose wheel. No ground school would teach my solution, which was inspired by what I had learned about ballast in Patrick O'Brian's book *Master and Commander*. Anyone who'd ever seen a teeter-totter could have thought of it. I loaded 20-pound boulders into the cargo compartment until the nose wheel levitated off the sand. I squeezed my frame into the cargo compartment and squatted over the rocks like a mother goose incubating her eggs. I was unaccompanied, undaunted, and unstrapped in the extreme rear of what was probably the most underpowered *Caravan* in the State of Alaska. Surely the Reaper was drooling with anticipation.

The "Boulder Plan," in a nutshell, was for me to heave boulders out of the cargo door as fast as possible while we accelerated down the beach to a speed at which the elevator would be sufficient to keep the nose gear from ploughing a furrow in the sand. After the last heave, I was to scurry forward to the safety of the cockpit.

I was no fortune teller, but I wasn't thrilled about my prospects. If Sasquatch rejected the takeoff while I was still in the back, I'd be beaten half-to-death like a bean bag in a tumble dryer. If I made it to the cockpit and he crashed into the rocks because the props couldn't hack it, I'd be mutilated *and* burned to a cinder like a cheap hot dog. Neither scenario had great appeal.

The only way I wouldn't be mutilated or cremated is if Sasquatch successfully made the takeoff. He poured the coal to the *Caravan* and I chucked boulders out the back like a maniac. We made it. As we limped away toward Anaktuvuk Pass, powered by misshapen and slightly vibrating propellers, Sasquatch asked me to mark the spot on a chart so he could bring his wife there for an idyllic picnic on some future day. He was a single minded guy, one not easily diverted from his mission.

With a little time remaining before our appointment in Anaktuvuk Pass, the boss dropped into Umiat, a small, isolated airport beside a river. He asked an airplane parts dealer who had set up shop there about buying a used *Caravan* propeller at a low, low price. The short answer was that he possessed neither a cheap *Caravan* propeller nor an expensive one. Sasquatch and I were highly-skilled airframe and power plant mechanics, so we filed the propeller blades as smoothly as we could before leaving Umiat.

Upon landing at Anaktuvuk Pass, I suggested rotating the three-bladed prop with the starter motor to a position that hid the bent prop tips from view of our passengers for fear of sapping their confidence.

"I like the way you think, young man."

Sasquatch had a way of making a young aviator feel good about himself even while he was committing acts of enormous stupidity. I was pleased that I had made the most out of a bad situation by impressing the chief pilot with my innovative approach to problem-solving. The incident taught me that teamwork was at the core of success.

Sasquatch confessed everything – almost everything -- to the owner, who, amazingly, let Sasquatch keep his job. I'm happy to report that I kept my job, too.

Six months later, I was still alive and flying a *Twin Otter* with a salty captain named "Indian Joe" McCoy. Indian Joe had flown for the CIA in Laos during the war, so he was fearless. Our mission was to fly through or over the Brooks Range to Anaktuvuk Pass (again) to pick up a high school basketball team. In the heart of winter at the 68th parallel, the sun was AWOL for 72 days. We had only a couple of hours of twilight to get the job done, so Joe's shortcut through a valley seemed entirely reasonable to me.

Weather closed in on us as we threaded our way above a river that was walled by mountains of over 7,000 feet in elevation. Joe told me not to worry, because he knew these mountains like the back of his hand. If so, he was the only person in the airplane who knew anything about this mountain range. They could have been the Alps for all I knew. As we muddled along, visibility fell to a number close to zero. I felt an uneasy quiver in my groin.

"I don't know about this," I said.

"No worries. I got it," he assured me.

A short time later, with forward visibility worse than it was before, it occurred to me that the altimeter was probably reading higher than actual because of sub-freezing temperatures. This thought fertilized my doubts.

"I don't know," I said. My voice seemed higher this time, possibly because my guts were churning like cottage cheese in a food processor.

"Got it," Joe said.

When I couldn't restrain my fears for a second longer, I said, "Joe, let's get the hell out of here!" I said it with conviction and regret – regret that I hadn't said it five minutes earlier.

Reluctantly, Joe added full power and turned right to reverse course. His eyes never penetrated the snowy gray sky to see the sheer cliff of slate and snow that popped out of the murk of twilight directly in front of us, but mine did. (My vision recently had been certified at 20/10, and my young, razor sharp peepers detected a mountainside looming in living black-and-white before Joe had a clue.)

I grabbed the yoke, slammed the throttles to the firewall, and tightened the right-hand turn. Joe got a late glimpse of the peak as it passed below his left leg.

"Close," he said.

Close? I guessed that being shot at on the Ho Chi Minh Trail had permanently skewed his measuring stick of danger. He resumed control of the aircraft while I dealt with heart palpitations and breathing anomalies.

A number of questions occupied my mind. Exactly how poor was Joe's vision? Just how well did he really know these mountains? How well did he know the back of his hand? How did I know that Joe wasn't thinking of some other mountain range? It was just a high school basketball game at stake: couldn't they show a little class and forfeit? Or maybe reschedule the game?

Just at that moment, from the bowl of milk in front of us, a second mountain peak seemed to lunge out at us. Joe uttered the Lord's name in vain and broke hard right to avoid impact. Miraculously, we missed smashing to bits on the second mountain, too! Every muscle in my body was as rigid as steel. I was so tensed up that I don't know why ligaments didn't tear or blood vessels rupture.

"Let's get out of here!" I said again. I didn't care what Joe thought of me anymore. I wanted to live. I wanted to be there for the children I hadn't yet conceived and to grow old with the wife I hadn't yet met.

Joe continued climbing at maximum power on instruments. Out of the whiteout, a third mountain peak appeared. It was like we had been transported to the middle of the Himalayas! Joe pulled the nose up and the airspeed indicator dropped alarmingly. I imagined splattering against the snowy cliff and sliding backwards into the abyss. We gained a little altitude but continued closer toward the craggy ridgeline. I had a new vision of slamming against the rock face and tumbling over into the abyss on the other side of the mountain. I didn't have time to pray for a third miracle. Straining to climb on the props, the airplane shuddered slightly as Joe kept back pressure on the controls. We were a caribou's eyelash from a stall.

The aircraft lurched violently when we hit. The collision injured Joe's left knee. Tuning knobs flew off the radios. As we burst into clear air on the other side of the mountain, I could see that the right wing tip was damaged. We were still sort of flying, but Joe was struggling to hold full left aileron to maintain wings level.

The missing knobs made it impossible to change frequencies on the navigation radio, so I used a pair of pliers to tune in a Point Barrow radio beacon that we could steer toward. It was our only means of navigation. Joe looked haggard.

"Need anything?" I asked.

"Apple juice."

I rummaged around in search of a container of apple juice. Consistent with the trend of our fortunes, the apple juice was frozen.

"Shit," Joe said.

Even though the collision had wiped the radio antennas off the aircraft, the transmitter/receiver was still operable at short range. Joe established radio contact with a bush pilot named Price Brower who was flying a *Caravan* in clear air nearby. Like the United States Cavalry, he soon arrived to help us. We continued to stagger north-northwesterly toward Point Barrow while Brice looked us over. He reported that the outermost one-third of our right wing was fluttering like a flag in the breeze and that our right main landing gear was missing.

This gloomy appraisal was especially disappointing to me. Except for the bent prop episode last summer, I had never put a scratch on an airplane before. Slamming against a mountain was so far outside my concept of flying that I questioned my basic premise of coming to Alaska. Brice got busy on the radio and gave us some more bad news.

Dead Horse, our nearest divert field, was blanketed by clouds and snow. The only airports that weren't similarly shut down were Point Barrow and, three miles away from that, a Naval Research air strip. At least that simplified our choice of destinations.

As we slow-flighted our way toward Point Barrow, I couldn't shake the feeling that the right wing was liable to fold up like an ironing board at any moment. I pondered how close I had come to becoming a harp-player. Brice flew on ahead of us to alert emergency responders of our pending arrival. Joe performed controllability checks to see how the plane would act at approach speeds. He didn't lower flaps for fear that they might extend unevenly and really ruin our day.

"I coulda used an apple juice," he said.

I offered to sit on the juice to thaw it out, but Joe said that wasn't necessary.

"We're going to be just fine," Joe predicted. His optimism truly knew no limits. "We'll land on the gravel strip at the Naval Research airport to avoid sparks, and we'll be just fine."

Fire trucks and an ambulance were waiting for us. Joe landed ever so gently, first on the left main gear, then the nose gear, then, when the right wing ran out of lift, the right wing stub fluttered to the runway. I had shut off fuel to the engines just before touchdown and then killed all electrical power, so we wouldn't immolate ourselves. At the end of our abbreviated ground run, punctuated by Joe's vigorous application of left wheel braking, the airplane skidded 90 degrees right to a hockey stop in the middle of the runway.

As a light swirl of dry snow blew over our two-legged *Twin Otter* like a magic puff of tiny crystals in the dusk, Joe and I just sat there for a moment, two grateful bush pilots, happy to have slipped out of the Grim Reaper's grasp.

Photo courtesy of Robert Shumaker

Robert "Bob" Shumaker

New Wilmington, Pennsylvania
United States Naval Academy
Rear Admiral, United States Navy
Eight-year Prisoner-of-War
T-34, T-28, T2V, F9F, SNB,
T-2A, F-8, B-52, KC-135
C-152, C-172, Cadet, Arrow,
Seminole, Debonair, Glasair
Associate Dean, University of North Dakota

CHAPTER 5

GLITCHES

DURING MY FIRST YEAR of flying the Navy's hottest new fighter, the F-8 *Crusader*, I learned two things about the Grim Reaper: first, he'll claim a victim at high speed, low speed, or no speed at all and, second, he'll string together a chain of glitches a mile long to get a victim.

On my sixth syllabus hop as a Lieutenant in VF-174 at Cecil Field near Jacksonville, Florida, I was briefed to climb to 45,000 feet to set up for a supersonic run that would earn me the right to wear a 1,000-mile-an-hour pin. A lot of bad things can happen going that fast, but, as I was about to learn, slow speed was no ticket to risk-free flying, either. An instructor named Lieutenant "Doc" Townsend flew on my wing as I attempted to climb over high cumulous clouds that jutted into the sky over Gainesville, Florida. "Doc," by the way, wasn't a real medical doctor, although he may have preferred to be one before this action-packed flight was over.

The thunderstorms in our path were building fast, so I had to pull back on the stick a tad to scoot up on top of them. As the airspeed continued to bleed off and as "Doc" figured out that we weren't going to have enough energy to clear the storm clouds, he radioed for me to reverse course. My airspeed had decayed to about 220 knots, just a few knots above stall speed. Of course, as soon as I banked the airplane, the *Crusader* stalled, fell into the angry clouds and, soon after that, was spinning at 200 degrees a second. Each 360 degrees of spin put me 1,400 feet closer to drilling a smoking hole in North Florida.

Flying on instruments, with no visual references at all, it took me 14 revolutions to complete the spin recovery procedure – power back, rudder against the spin, ailerons into the spin direction, and blow down the wing leading edge devices with an emergency air bottle. At one point during my wild ride 20,000 feet down the shaft of tumbling cumulus, flames were shooting out of the intake just below my feet like fire from a dragon's mouth. Mildly amazed when the procedure actually worked, I recovered in the clouds on instruments and managed to fly out unscathed into clear air. I didn't earn my 1,000-miles-an-hour pin that day, but the Grim Reaper didn't get a trophy, either.

Later that year, while deployed with VF-32, the "Sonic Swordsmen," aboard *USS Saratoga* in the Mediterranean, I again encountered the Reaper's skullduggery. Close to the end of a night air combat patrol mission in the middle of the "Med," I was headed back toward *Saratoga* with visions in my head of enjoying a late dinner followed by teaching my good friend and roommate Bill Adams a few new guitar chords. The Reaper had other plans.

Glitch Number One occurred when my tail hook refused to extend. Without a tail hook, I had no way to snag one of the six arresting cables stretched across the deck of the ship. I touched down onto the deck on three approaches, but each time the hook failed to fall into position. After my third bolter, the Air Boss directed me to divert to Italy.

Glitch Number Two was that I didn't have enough fuel to divert to an air base on any land mass in the world, including Italy. The Air Boss had a back-up plan; he radioed for me to join up with an A-4 *Skyhawk* inflight refueling tanker overhead and take on the fuel I needed to reach Italy.

It was a spectacular plan, but, when I joined up on the tanker, I discovered another glitch.

Glitch Number Three was that the tanker couldn't deploy the refueling hose. He had lots of gas, but I couldn't get any of it. I had only five minutes of fuel remaining when the Air Boss cheered me up by announcing that our crack deck crew was rigging a barricade. Outstanding! A barricade was a sort of tennis net on steroids strung between two industrial-strength stanchions. Landing into a barricade would damage the aircraft but it would protect me from becoming a supersonic submarine captain. I could live with a little damage to my *Crusader*. What had it done for me recently?

Glitch Number Four didn't completely surprise me because I was getting accustomed to glitches. The stanchions wouldn't erect to the vertical position even with the assistance of powerful tractors. The barricade might have been the finest of its kind in the United States Navy, but it wouldn't have done me any good lying on the deck. Down on *Saratoga*, my commanding officer sprinted from the wardroom to the tower in time to tell me to eject. Ejection is a procedure where a fighter pilot transitions from a warm cockpit through a violent rush of wind to a frigid ocean with an unpredictable, often thrilling parachute ride in between. No one was ever eager to punch out, but ejecting was almost always better than the alternative. The engine kept running until I had climbed to 4,000 feet. When the fuel ran out and the jet got quiet, I pulled the face curtain down over my helmet. Luckily, the seat fired and I became a projectile tumbling rapidly through an ebony sky over a forbidding ocean as big as infinity.

Glitch Number Five surfaced quickly thereafter. The parachute was supposed to open automatically, but it didn't. Falling in blackness toward the cold, inhospitable depths of the Mediterranean was enough to alarm even the most intrepid aviator, and it certainly alarmed me. Fortunately, my brain was working at double-time, and I remembered that I could pull an alternative parachute deployment device called the "D-ring."

Glitch Number Six: the "D-ring" didn't function. The Reaper had me right where he wanted me – hurtling toward the ocean just two thousand feet below me. Thoughts of smashing onto the surface of the sea made me momentarily the strongest man in the world. I yanked the "D-ring" with all the force I could muster and the parachute deployed!

Things started looking up then. I think the Reaper just gave up. I hit the water without loss of life and a destroyer plucked my bruised and soaking wet body out of the sea. The destroyer transferred me back to *Saratoga* on a "boatswain's chair," which would have been my last choice of transportation mode that evening.

My squadron mates were on deck to welcome me back. Bill, my afore-mentioned roommate, in a stunt obviously intended to taunt the Grim Reaper, was wearing my Stetson hat and my cowboy boots. Such integrity! (A lesser man who had written me off too quickly would have slinked back to the state room to replace my cherished attire.) Bill's timing may have been slightly off, but his instincts were good, and his friendship was priceless.

Rear Admiral Robert Shumaker's adventures flying off *USS Saratoga* were featured in Ron Knott's book *Supersonic Cowboys*. Admiral Shumaker was the second United States Navy fighter pilot shot down and confined by the North Vietnamese during the Vietnam War. Upon his release after eight years of imprisonment, Admiral Shumaker achieved distinction as a senior flag officer and a college associate dean.

Photo credit: focuspocusltd/depositphotos.com

Anonymous
From Somewhere in Texas
University of Hard Knocks
Undisclosed Rank, United States Air Force
F-4, F-16, F-15

CHAPTER 6

BORKUM

I WAS HOMEOPATHICALLY treating my Hawaiian sunburn with gin down on Waikiki Beach at the Fort DeRussy Officers Club bar. It was the early Seventies and drinks were cheap, maybe 25 cents. The only other guy at the bar was a lean, almost gaunt guy about five years older than me. He was dressed in khaki shorts and top-siders, and he sported a Robin Olds handlebar mustache.

"You're glowing," he said.

His comment was more of a medical assessment than a compliment.

"Fell asleep on the beach. Jet lag."

The man ordered a glass of neat *Sheep Dip*, a Scottish single malt of considerable merit. He was a handsome dude. Thirsty, too. He downed the *Dip* quickly, like he didn't have much time. He told me he was a medically retired Navy F-8 *Crusader* pilot.

I was a fighter pilot, too, only I was in the Air Force, so I didn't tell him right away because I knew how touchy Navy pilots can be about Air Force air-conditioners, long runways, and primo golf courses. His speech was less prosaic than it was philosophical.

"The Grim Reaper can get you just as easy on the ground as in the air," he said gravely.

I assumed that he'd figured out that I was a pilot. He had, no doubt, taken note of traits that two martinis reveal in me – a rapier-sharp intellect and the lightning-fast reflexes of a jaguar. There again, maybe it was my Rolex watch that gave me away. He didn't ask whether I was Navy or Air Force.

"Common misconception," he said. "Pilots don't die just in the air." On that cheerful note, he extended his hand. "Borkum." His handshake was a vice grip, but I held my own.

"That a family name or a call sign?"

"Call sign."

He told me the long version of how he got his call sign, but, well into my third martini, I didn't fully follow the story line. I just remember that it involved a Navy Captain's daughter and a hammock at Miramar.

"You can't dodge the Reaper forever," he said.

Sensing that he was on the verge of presenting supporting evidence, I paid for another *Dip* for Borkum.

"Borkum … cool call sign," I said.

"Gotta have a cool call sign or you're dicked." He gazed affectionately into the amber depths of his new *Dip*. "My squadron had … let's see … guys named Gator, Maggot, Taco, Buzzard … Porky, Crusher, Brillo, and Tex."

He rattled off the names as though his memories of them were fresh. I told him the righteous call signs in my last squadron, too: Bam Bam, Cisco, Rim Shot, Tupelo, Ruger, Marmaduke, Live Bait, Tonto, Diablo, Bazooka, and Tex.

"Everybody's got a Tex. Figured you were a pilot."

The thing was this: Borkum was a combat veteran; I was not. He was a man of war; I was a man of peace. While he was getting the crap shot out of him in Southeast Asia, I was beaming around Europe fulfilling my role in a socio-military outfit called USAFE, pronounced "you-safe-ee", the United States Air Forces in Europe.

My expertise lay in the area of wine, food, and a smattering of prominent Indo-European languages. I could, for example, ask, "Please direct me to my hotel," in Spanish, French, Italian, and even German. (The difference in these languages, by the way, was that a Spaniard or an Italian would actually take time to help me find my hotel. A citizen of France or Germany, on the other hand, couldn't give a flying fart whether I ever found my hotel.)

The point was that I considered it best to keep my mouth shut and listen to the man of war tell the man of peace a thing or two about fighter pilots *vis-á-vis* the Grim Reaper.

"Next thing," Borkum said, "you have to know where the cool clubs are. Ever been to Subic Bay?"

I could find Subic Bay on a map of the Philippines, but that wasn't what the man had asked me.

"No."

"Or the *Dragonboat Bar* at the Hong Kong Hilton?"

"Never been there."

"The Cubi Point O Club ... ahh ... it was beyond great." Sip of *Dip*. "Maggott broke ... that thing ... hangs from the ceiling?"

"Trapeze," I said, messing with him.

"Other thing."

"Chandelier."

"Maggot broke the O Club chandelier trying to do a Tarzan thing ... a swing." He snorted at the memory, and I could tell that the *Dip* burned his nose coming back up. "We all chipped in to pay for it."

I'd done the same thing when Tuna had clowned around and broken the chandelier in the O Club at Aviano, but I kept the recollection to myself. I didn't snort like Borkum, either, saving myself a sinus burn.

"And Crusher won over five hundred dollars eating a light bulb at the *East Inn Club* in Olongapo. He didn't swallow the thing ...."

"The filament."

"The filament ... or the metal."

I didn't pass judgment. When guys got together after flying, anything was possible. I once saw a guy eat a light bulb on a bet at the Ramstein O Club. He was a Lieutenant. I always wondered whether he made Captain. He was probably a lot smarter in the air than he was on the ground. On the other hand, the German beer probably made him a lot braver on the ground than he was in the air.

"Did you ever think the Grim Reaper was gonna get you?" I asked.

Borkum laughed. "Yeah ... the first time I flew over Hanoi. I almost shit a brick when I saw a friggin' SA-2 launch. It guided on me and it got so close that I almost passed another brick while I was doing my half-assed SAM break. Two bricks in less than a minute." He used his hands to show how the missile had overshot his *Crusader*. "Then the triple-A just about tattooed a number on me. Good thing you can only get so scared, otherwise the damage could've been permanent. How about you? Ever taste adrenalin?"

I *had* tasted adrenalin, but my story about hitting trees on a low level in the mountains and bringing back pine tree boughs tangled up in the triple ejection rack (TER) on the left wing of my F-4 *Phantom* wasn't in the same league as getting hosed by surface-to-air missiles and 37-mike-mike.

"I've tasted it," I said. "Like licking the inside of a tin can. Or a cheap harmonica."

"Prob'ly don't know how close you came to buying the farm. Most pilots should be dead three or four times over."

"Probably," I said. I remembered my knees buckling on the ground when I spotted the flora jammed into my left

TER. At 600 knots, I would have died *muy rapidamente* if I'd been a couple of feet lower. I remembered my hand shaking when I signed the post-flight forms.

"The Reaper never got me in the air, but now that sorry son-of-a-bitch is taking a shot at me on the ground. Damn prostrate!"

He had put in an *R* that didn't belong there. He was probably an engineer. Stanford or Georgia Tech was my guess. None of the engineers I had ever flown with could spell worth a lick. Guys with cancer of the prostate who mispronounced "prostate" kept on mispronouncing it, because who was going to criticize a guy with cancer? Who cares about spelling when you're dying? As I said, engineers don't care about spelling even when they're *living*.

"Are you getting treatment?" I asked.

"The quacks have barbequed up my nuts like an overdone brisket. I'm sick of it." He fidgeted with his zipper and, for a second, I feared that he was going to resort to a visual aid like President Lyndon Johnson displaying his gall bladder incision to reporters. No worries: Borkum was just scratching like baseball players do when they're in the batter's box. "Not much longer now."

"I'm sorry," I told him.

"No sweat. I'm overdue. I flew a hundred-and-two missions up North, so the Reaper shoulda bagged my ass then. I'm not complaining." His tone was flippant, but his eyes were moist.

He was too good looking to die, I thought. It didn't seem fair, seeing as how he had been through so much already. But that was the thing about the Reaper ... he always got you in the end.

"I'm real sorry, Borkum." My eyes were moist, too.

He squeezed the last drop out of his glass of *Dip* and shrugged his shoulders.

"I had a damn good run," he said. "Better to die than look bad."

That was a lot of years ago. I think about Borkum sometimes. He's long gone by now, but I'm glad I met him that night at Fort DeRussy. Sometimes I toast him with whatever I'm drinking … seems like they never have *Sheep Dip* anymore. And I whisper the words of an old fighter pilot song:

God bless the fighter pilots who roar into the blue,
Taunting the Grim Reaper 'till he comes to get his due.

The writer, like Borkum, also suffered from prostate cancer later in life. He never did get back to Fort DeRussy.

Photo courtesy of G. H. Spaulding

G. H. "Spud" Spaulding

Colorado Springs, Colorado
BA, Southern Colorado State College
MPA, George Washington University
Captain, United States Navy
P-3, T-44, TS-2, T-28,
T-34, USAF C-12

CHAPTER 7

STORM

THE GRIM REAPER can end a pilot's career without killing him. The grisly executioner punishes survivors, too.

A man inserts a key into the lock of the front door of a single-story concrete building not far from Naval Air Station Whiting Field, Florida. The engine roar of a Navy T-28 *Trojan* is a familiar sound to him, but he's never heard a *Trojan* engine howl so loudly before. He whips his head around in time to see a *Trojan*, upside-down and streaming condensation trails from its prop tips, hurtling straight toward him. Terrified, the man leaps away from the building a second before the aircraft impacts, explodes, and smashes the building into rubble.

In my role as a Navy flight instructor, I routinely flew four T-28 flights a day to train Basic stage Navy pilot candidates. Demand was high because of escalating combat in Vietnam. My call sign was "Two Whiskey Triple Sticks." I got the name from the tail number of the T-28 assigned to me – "2W-111."

On the morning of the crash, a steady northeast wind chased wispy powder-puff clouds across a pale blue sky. The puffy clouds were standard Florida Panhandle fare until they reached the Gulf of Mexico. There, only a few miles south of Whiting Field, the benign clouds collided with an invisible barrier, doubled back, and churned like curdled cream in a mixer. Throughout the morning, an unstable white curtain of clouds continued to build up just south of the coastline.

Ensign McCauley was my student pilot that morning. He had a reputation for being smooth and confident in the T-28. In an unusual twist of fate, McCauley and his good college buddy had married sisters. The recent college graduates, now brothers-in-law, had been accepted into Navy pilot training at the same time. It was a rare bonus for brothers-in-law to be able to study together and support one another in pursuit of naval aviator wings.

McCauley was scheduled to fly under a hood in my back seat on a syllabus-required instrument training flight. The hood was a white, accordion-like canvas curtain that, when pulled forward, obscured the rear pilot's exterior vision as though by the cover of a Conestoga wagon. Cocooned by the hood, McCauley had to rely completely on instruments to fly the aircraft.

He executed the climb to 13,000 feet perfectly. To allow me to scan for possible conflicts, he made constant clearing turns of precisely thirty degrees either side of our navigational course. His airspeed, rate of climb, and rate of turn were all on the money. McCauley had what we called "good hands." During the instrument mission, I maintained a careful watch for conflicting traffic. Although the weather was good in our immediate area, a radio transmission confirmed that adverse weather was building behind us.

"This is Whiting Tower on Guard. Whiting Field is now closed for a runway change. The new duty runway will be *Runway Two-Two*."

The wind had shifted dramatically from the northeast to the southwest in less than three minutes. Such a sudden reversal of winds frequently preceded deteriorating weather. I was concerned that we might have to divert to an alternate landing field. We might even get stuck there for the night. I assumed control of the aircraft, told McCauley to "pop the bag" (retract the hood), and I headed the aircraft back toward home base. Ten minutes later, I reported on initial at Whiting Field. The controller cleared me number five for the break to downwind.

Poor visibility made it hard to see other aircraft in the visual pattern. McCauley and I counted aircraft carefully, so I could take interval on the fourth one. Just outside the boundary of a massive thunderstorm, as I started our turn to downwind leg, a T-28 flying in the opposite direction darted out of the clouds and flashed by my canopy. Closing speed of the two aircraft was over 240 knots, so it happened fast. The startling sight of the other *Trojan* passing less than six feet over my canopy made me duck reflexively.

"Close," McCauley said.

Truly, I don't know how we avoided being hit by the other *Trojan*. I landed "Triple Sticks" in a heavy downpour, taxied through buffeting winds and intense rain to the ramp, and shut down the engine. The rain was blowing almost horizontally, and McCauley and I got soaked as we dashed from "Triple Sticks" to the hangar. Inside, we got news that a *Trojan* had gone down in the storm. When the storm cell passed and the rain slackened, the visibility improved and we could see a column of black smoke rising from a stand of pines near my off-base home. Of course, I was worried for the safety of my wife Ev and our children Scott and Brian. McCauley asked if he might join me as I headed for my car to drive to the crash site. A few minutes later, I was relieved to discover that the burning wreckage was a safe distance from our neighborhood.

Weeks later, an accident board concluded that the student pilot of the crashed *Trojan* had become disoriented after losing sight of his formation leader in the roiling clouds that had invaded the skies over Whiting Field. An instructor pilot in a chase plane had followed him during lost wingman procedures but had been unable to restore the student's orientation. The formation leader, also a student pilot, had been flying the aircraft that had narrowly missed our *Trojan*. Despite the near-miss, he had remained spatially oriented and he had safely recovered his aircraft.

At the accident site, McCauley and I remained clear of rescue efforts. We were silent, dismayed. A search-and-rescue helicopter hovered over the crash site like a humming bird, its rotor blades whipping the column of black smoke that billowed from the inferno then swirled into the rain and thickened the ominous overcast. Yellow fire engines and crash trucks pumped torrents of fire suppressant chemicals onto the flames. I contemplated how McCauley and I had dodged the same fate by less than two yards. Members of the crash crew in heavy asbestos suits waded into hot, smoky piles of debris and removed the horribly charred and decapitated body of the student pilot. McCauley and I somberly returned to my car for the drive back to base. I dropped McCauley at his car.

"See you tomorrow, Sir," he said. He rendered a salute and then turned away in the light rain to unlock his car.

The following day, McCauley didn't report for his scheduled flight briefing. I never saw him again. Because of the crash's traumatic effect, the talented young aviator had forsaken his quest for Navy wings. I felt intense empathy for him when I learned that the burned and mutilated corpse recovered from the burning *Trojan* was the body of McCauley's brother-in-law.

G. H. Spaulding is the author of three books: *C-C-Cold War Syndrome*, *Takeout*, and *Decree*. They are available on Amazon.

Photo courtesy of H. C. Stevenson

Steve "Cowboy" Stevenson

Bulverde, Texas
University of Texas
Auburn University
Captain, United States Army
Colonel, United States Air Force
F-4, CT-39, A-10, O-2, OT-37 OV-10,
Alpha Jet, CH-3, MH-60
Just about every Cessna up to *Citation X*

CHAPTER 8

SNOW

"COWBOY, PULL UP!"

Slam throttles forward. Yank stick aft. Canopy filled by a snow-bound farmhouse, bleached, bathed in brilliant white. Death-minus-one-second. The Grim Reaper called my name.

A bitter cold front had roared across the British Isles all night and had dumped heavy snow on the Scottish Highlands. The front pushed showers of wintery mix as far south as RAF Bentwaters in Suffolk County (northeast of London). Bentwaters was home base to my A-10 squadron. The A-10 was the finest close-air support, low-altitude-environment airplane in the world. Fairchild Republic, manufacturer of the A-10, officially named it A-10 *Thunderbolt*. Pilots like me who loved flying the A-10 dubbed it *Warthog*, or, simply, *Hog*.

I was scheduled to fly as *Skull Two-One*, leading a two-ship of A-10s on a sortie that included aerial refueling, two Electronic Warfare Tactics Range runs, and lots of low-level navigation on the way back to the home drome. My wingman, *Skull Two-Two*, was a top-notch *Hog* Driver named Captain Kevin "Oats" Barley. I didn't have to tell Oats that the blanket of snow would make the low level navigation a challenge-and-a-half. I had no premonition that this was to be one of those days that I almost bought the farm.

After taking off from Bentwaters, Oats and I climbed up uneventfully to a refueling track well off the east coast of Scotland to rendezvous with a KC-135 tanker, *Dobby One-One*. In clear air at Flight Level 230, well above the wintry mess down below, we got a tally-ho on *Dobby,* established in the track headed toward us. I called *Dobby's* turn on the radio, and he rolled out two minutes later five hundred feet precisely above us. Perfect. Oats flew up to an observation position on the tanker's right wing while I flew smartly up to pre-contact position, the refueling nozzle right in front of my canopy. I opened the refueling door, located five feet in front of my face, and gently advanced a single throttle to slide forward about three feet to stabilize in contact position. The boom operator extended the boom until the nozzle locked into my receptacle with a "thunk." The fuel began to flow into my jet. I made tiny throttle and trim adjustments to account for the changes in aircraft weight and center of gravity. The boom operator didn't have to say a word. When I had received my allocated load of JP-4, the boom operator disconnected, and I flew up and left off the tanker's left-wing tip. Oats moved smoothly down toward the nozzle, stabilized, and got plugged by the boom operator. When Oats had received his pre-briefed fuel load, the boom operator disconnected and partially retracted the boom. At disconnect, about a gallon of fuel sprayed onto Oats's canopy, briefly blocking his forward vision. Routine. We repeated the cycle. Done. We each had received two thousand pounds of fuel and a free canopy wash. As we cleared off the tanker, I transmitted on the radio.

"*Dobby One-One*, thanks for the gas. *Skull Two-One* Flight's clear, down, and left. *Two-One*, Button Nine, go."

"*Two*," Oates acknowledged.

We checked in on the UHF radio frequency reserved for the RAF Spadeadam Range Control.

"*Skull Two-One*, check."

"*Two*."

We descended westward and coasted-in north of Newcastle upon Tyne for our two passes on the tactics range located north of Hadrian's Wall not far from the borders of Cumbria County, Northumberland County, and Scotland.

"Spadeadam, *Skull Two-One*, two A-Tens with you, forty miles east for two scheduled runs at ten-fifteen hours."

In a wonderful Scottish brogue, the controller replied, "*Skull Two-One*, Spadeadam, you're cleared onto the range at IP Number Three. Altimeter two-niner-niner-eight."

"Two-niner-niner-eight and *Skull* is cleared onto the range," I said.

"*Two*."

The sun reflected brilliantly off the fresh layer of snow. Oats flexed into a 2,500-foot wedge formation as we flew about four-hundred feet over a snow-covered forest. The tall trees gave me a good perspective of our height above the ground. We needed to stay low enough to avoid detection by Royal Air Force radars simulating Soviet air defense systems. My ALR-69 Radar Warning Receiver (RWR) soon came to life with audible beeps, chirps, and rattles. The RWR displayed symbols on a digital screen to identify specific threats and their bearings. Oats and I descended even lower to avoid detection. The world was covered by a white blanket, making it hard to estimate our height above the white blur of the terrain below. It was a busy time. My eyes were sweeping from inside the cockpit back outside to clear the trees flashing by just a few feet below my *Hog*. I hugged the valley floor and crossed the ridgelines as low as possible to remain invisible to the enemy. A radio transmission broke my concentration.

"Cowboy, Altitude!" Oats called on the radio, using my personal call sign.

My eyes snapped outside the cockpit. Filling my HUD gunsight and the windscreen, above the altitude of my *Hog*, was a farmhouse and a fieldstone wall!

"Cowboy, pull up!" Oats shouted even more urgently.

I yanked the stick back and shoved the throttles to the stops. The instantaneous *G* forces and engine exhaust blew snow on the ground into a blizzard that momentarily obscured the house and my aircraft from sight. I emerged from the frenzied cloud of snow knowing full well that, if I had pulled up a second or two later, I would have scattered A-10 parts all over Cumbria County!

With my attention focused on the RWR detection of sophisticated threats, I had failed to notice a more immediate, more primitive threat – the ground. This wasn't an example of not seeing the forest for the trees. This was a case of calibrating my height above ground relative to the height of one-hundred-foot-tall trees. The farmhouse wasn't surrounded by one-hundred-foot-tall trees; the farmhouse was in the middle of five-foot-tall bushes! My perspective of height above the ground was also distorted by the absence of visual details in the dazzling white landscape. Oats and I knew that I had narrowly escaped converting the seven barrels of my Gatling gun into snow cones.

I've thought back many times on the snowy day I dodged the Reaper. A pilot can die as quickly in training as in combat. I thank the Lord for Oats and other good wingmen like him who have kept me alive in both!

Harry C. Stevenson, Colonel, United States Air Force (Retired), is the author of *From Both Sides Now: Paratrooper, Green Beret, Fighter Pilot*. It is available on Amazon.

Photo credit: Christopher Fell, Andrew Oxley, & photogaphier/123RF.com

Melvyn Paisley

Umpqua River, Oregon
Lieutenant, United States Army Air Force
P-47 *Thunderbolt*

CHAPTER 9

LA MORT

AT THE BATTLE OF THE BULGE, the largest single battle on the Western Front during World War II, the Grim Reaper had his way for forty days of gory mayhem beginning on December 16, 1944. The sum of German casualties, missing, and captured exceeded 84,000; for the Americans, the figure was over 87,000. The Reaper took several swipes at First Lieutenant Melvyn Paisley, a P-47 *Thunderbolt* pilot assigned to the 390th Fighter Squadron.

Paisley was lucky to get back alive to his base at Asch, Belgium after bombing German anti-tank guns on Christmas Eve. Pulling off his target, his aircraft was hit by anti-aircraft fire. He nursed his P-47 (named *La Mort*) up to six thousand feet for the return to Asch. On descent over Liege, Belgium, he spotted a formation of four *Luftwaffe* Messerschmitt Me-109 fighters. He performed a split-S maneuver that positioned him behind the trailing Messerschmitt. Paisley fired two bursts of his eight .50-caliber guns, and the canopy of the Me-109 exploded. The three other German fighter planes scattered. Shortly after that encounter, Paisley's luck almost went AWOL when four British Hawker *Typhoons* mistook him for a German aircraft and attacked him. Luckily, none of the *Typhoons'* bullets found their marks. The Royal Air Force fighters recognized their mistake and bugged out, leaving Paisley to limp back to Asch running on

51

fumes. Because his right aileron had been damaged by shrapnel, Paisley's landing at Asch was far short of Landing of the Year.

Paisley was a Type A personality, and his Christmas Eve wasn't over by a long shot. While his crew chief patched up *La Mort*, Paisley persuaded a sergeant in the motor pool to transport him and some squadron buddies to a dance in the Belgian town of Hasselt. Their first stop was at a Belgian coal mine where local miners allowed Yank fighter pilots to take frigid showers in a rustic latrine. During Paisley's shower, someone stole his .45-caliber Colt. Disarmed but fragrant, Paisley valiantly pressed on. He made good use of excess capacity in the Army weapons carrier by picking up some Belgian girls at a café along the way. Upon arriving at the Hasselt town square, Paisley told the driver to remove the rotor from the distributor cap so guard duty wouldn't distract the sergeant from sampling local ales. Apparently a missing distributor cap was not an insurmountable obstacle to thieves, because, when the tipsy crew rendezvoused at the square at midnight, the truck had gone the way of Paisley's *Colt 45*. Paisley called the base to ask for a duty officer to pick them up for their return trip.

While waiting to be rescued, Paisley's most recent Belgian girlfriend led him around a corner to a barn that housed the shop of a blacksmith. Because Paisley was four inches shorter than the amorous lady, he had difficulty performing the standing maneuver she had in mind. He solved the problem by hopping on top of an anvil. Their passion mostly spent, Paisley and his war-time lover parted without knowing whether they would ever meet again.

A week later on New Year's Eve, Paisley was still very much alive and, because he had been selected to lead the Squadron's 12 P-47s into combat the following morning, he was also very much sober. It was a common misconception that pilots had to be snockered to sing salty traditional fighter pilot songs. In fact, as Paisley proved, (although he may not have been technically in-tune for every single note) a pilot can be quite sober while singing an old favorite to the melody of *If You're Happy And You Know It, Clap Your Hands!*

Oh, there are no fighter pilots down in hell.
Oh, there are no fighter pilots down in hell.
The place is full of queers, navigators, bombardiers,
But there are no fighter pilots down in hell.

Oh, there are no fighter pilots in the states.
Oh, there are no fighter pilots in the states.
They're off to foreign shores, making mothers out of whores,
Oh, there are no fighter pilots in the states.

The Americans and British flew over 17,500 sorties during the Battle of the Bulge, and the loss of Allied pilots was alarming. Paisley had no idea that the Grim Reaper was shrieking like a banshee beneath the winter moon in anticipation of a major New Year's Day attack that the German General Staff called the *Great Blow*. Early that morning, the *Luftwaffe* launched almost a thousand fighters against nine Allied airfields. Their first attack succeeded in destroying 20 Supermarine *Spitfires* on the ground at a nearby Royal Air Force base. The extra five minutes required for the *Luftwaffe* to reach Asch was crucial to Paisley's success.

When he saw a force of 80 German fighters flying at low level directly for Asch, Paisley jettisoned his bombs and engaged them like a rabid tiger. Using guns and rockets, Paisley quickly shot down five German fighters! His squadron mates were credited with seven more kills. Paisley's wingman shot down two Me-109s before being shot down himself. After landing near one of his victims, the downed American flier discovered that the dead German pilot was Lieutenant Colonel Guenther Specht, the JG-11 Squadron Commander and an ace with 32 victories. The wingman purloined Specht's pistol as a trophy.

The Germans lost more than 250 fighters along with several key commanders that day. Against great odds, Paisley's squadron lost only one pilot, a single P-47 in the air, and one P-47 on the ground. Paisley's banner day of frustrating the Grim Reaper had made him an ace!

Historical Addendum

Lt. Melvyn Paisley's 390th Fighter Squadron (FS) was inactivated along with the other squadrons in the 366th Fighter Wing (FW) after the end of the war in 1945. When the 366th FW was reactivated on January 1, 1953, the 390th FS was reconstituted as an integral part of the wing. At various times, 366th FW squadrons have flown front-line fighters such as the P-51 *Mustang*, F-86 *Sabre*, F-84 *Thunderjet*, F-100 *Super Sabre*, F-4 *Phantom*, and F-15 *Eagle* in succession at England Air Force Base , Louisiana; Chaumont-Semoutiers Air Base, France; Holloman Air Force Base, New Mexico; Phan Rang Air Base, South Vietnam; Da Nang Air Base, South Vietnam; Takhli Royal Thai Air Force Base, Thailand; and Mountain Home Air Force Base, Idaho.

Paisley, Melvyn. *ACE! Autobiography of a Fighter Pilot World War II*. Branden, 1992.

Photo courtesy of Tom Lee

Tom Lee

Louisville, Kentucky
Michigan State University
Major, United States Marine Corps
C-150, P-140, Saratoga, Cherokee 6,
Cheyenne, Falcon 10, Lear 35, *Citation*,
Bombardier CRJ200
Atlantic Coast Airlines

CHAPTER 10

SMOKE

YOW. That's the three-letter identifier for the Macdonald-Cartier International Airport near Ottawa, Canada. "YOW" amused me the first time I saw it on my schedule, but the humor didn't last. I was at YOW, waiting for the inbound captain to toss me the keys to a Bombardier CRJ200 so I could fly the last day of my four-day trip. (Attention, Non-flyers: Airliners don't really have keys. It's just a slang expression I've used to juice up my recollections of the day the Grim Reaper almost took me out.)

My crew and I were scheduled to block eight hours during our fourteen-hour duty period. Our reward was to be able to sleep in our own beds that night back home in Atlanta. The inbound captain mentioned a flickering caution light that had caught his attention but hadn't merited a write-up. Flickering caution lights were as common on CRJ200s as earthquakes were in California.

"It's like when a pretty girl winks at you," he said. "It's so quick that you're not sure it really happened."

I nodded sagely. I was pretty sure that the younger captain and I didn't hang out in the same circles. I had a wife, two kids, and a mortgage, so I encountered winking pretty girls about as frequently as lunar eclipses. I watched alertly through engine start, taxi, takeoff, and climb, but there were no flickering caution lights that I could see. There were no winking pretty girls, either, although, at top-of-climb, the flight attendant did bring up steaming hot cups of coffee for me and Dave, my first officer. Someone somewhere had convinced the flight attendant that pilots love nothing more than molten lava in a cup. She had double-cupped the coffees, but, really, she was negligent for failing to affix hazardous materials warning labels to the cups as well. Through all of this *petit drame*, no caution lights, flickering or otherwise.

"Yow!" Dave said after scalding himself.

"Yow" – YOW. I got it. I'd always had a lot of respect for guys who could find comedy in the face of adversity. No doubt about it, Dave had a lot of potential.

The first leg to Atlanta was uneventful. So was the second to LaGuardia. And the third to Cleveland. The flickering caution light was a distant memory, filed in the farthest reaches of my sub-consciousness. One leg to go: Cleveland to Atlanta and home. In the pitch black of midnight, I could see a stream of airliners' landing lights stretching like Christmas tree lights for fifty miles toward Hartsfield, Atlanta's major airport. We were about to cross "Rome" waypoint on the Earlin STAR (arrival).

"Do you smell something?" Dave asked.

I sure did. As though on Dave's command, the cockpit immediately filled with thick, acrid smoke.

"Mask!" I shouted.

Faster and more graceful than a gazelle on the Serengeti, Dave donned his oxygen mask in about one-point-five nanoseconds. I was a tad slower on the draw. If it had been a gun fight, Dave would have won and I would have been lying in a pool of blood on Dodge City's main street.

I digress.

I gasped, trying not to inhale the foul fumes. My oxygen hose was wrapped around my oxygen mask like a ball of yarn after a cat's played with it. I shouted for Dave to run the appropriate emergency procedure checklist while I wrestled with the oxygen mask like Indiana Jones grappling with a boa constrictor. Finally I got the mask on and took a lung-full of one-hundred-per-cent-pure made-in-America oxygen.

The trick to speaking with an oxygen mask clamped onto your face is to treat it like a scuba mask: inhale, talk, exhale. If you did it any other way, your transmission would be just unintelligible heavy breathing, like the sound of hippos mating. We were barreling in on the Earlin Arrival toward Atlanta, the busiest airport on the planet, so I had to say something. I radioed to Atlanta Approach Control that I was declaring an emergency for smoke in the cockpit. The radio frequency got unusually quiet. The controller never missed a beat. He came back with distances to Atlanta and to Chattanooga and asked me to state my intentions. "State your intentions" is another way for a controller to tell a pilot, "If you haven't got a plan, you better get one pretty quick." My plan was to divert to Chattanooga because it was closer, and, judging by the dense smoke filling the cockpit, there might not be that much time remaining before this flight segment was history. The controller assigned me a heading and cleared me for the approach to Chattanooga. He even cleared me to land. How's that for service?

The cockpit was like the inside of a smoke stack. I couldn't see outside the aircraft at all. I could barely make out the instruments. We were descending through 11,000 feet and scooting along at 320 knots. Each time the controller radioed my distance from the Chattanooga airport, I reminded him that I couldn't see anything. Perhaps it was a subtle plea for pity. He notified me of alternate landing places like an interstate highway to my left, a small road to my right, a little airport over there. I had never landed on a highway or gone screaming off the end of a stubby little runway before, and I certainly didn't want to start a new trend that night.

I told Dave to tune in the Chattanooga Runway Three-Six ILS frequency. Faster than a cheetah on a Tanzanian savanna, Dave had the ILS tuned in. I still couldn't see out of the cockpit, but the instruments told me I was too high, too fast, and generally in no position to conduct a normal approach to the Chattanooga Metropolitan Airport. I needed to get the plane on the ground as fast as possible. This was no time for go-arounds or three-sixties, so, the moment I got a glimpse of the ground, I improvised by pulling out a maneuver from an especially dark place. Only a certified maniac would have approved of my idea. I aggressively raised the nose of the aircraft and extended the flight spoilers. I say "aggressively," but not so "aggressively" as to yank the wings off the airplane. I needed the wings to stay attached for a few more minutes. Gear down, flaps full, stow the spoilers, flare, touchdown. It was a magically smooth touchdown for a guy who could barely see through the windscreen. We rolled off the runway into the middle of a circle of 14 firetrucks. (A lot of towns don't have that many fire trucks in their Fourth of July parades.)

I set the parking brake and allowed my vibrating knees time to settle down. I had just performed a number of aerial maneuvers for the first time in my life, and I needed time to process what I'd seen and *not* seen. Good old Dave was running a checklist as fast as … some kind of wild animal in some remote part of the earth. He was a marvel.

When my legs had stopped shaking, I stood up on them and I opened the flight deck door to step into the main cabin. The passengers had a right to know what the hell was going on. A cloud of heavy smoke rolled out from behind me up over my head into the cabin. For only a second, perhaps because of a psychologically exotic form of suppressed hysteria camouflaged by a cool exterior, I imagined running onto a football field during team introductions at the Super Bowl -- smoke billowing around me, fireworks exploding in all quadrants, and a gaggle of jets roaring over the stadium in a flyby that boosted the crowd into a state of frenzy.

I imagined the announcer saying, "And, now, playing captain, from Michigan State University, it's ...." (I would like to emphasize that the delusion lasted only for a second ... or two.)

The look of terror in my passengers' eyes told me that I needn't elaborate on the circumstances that had brought us to Chattanooga. Smoke generally spoke for itself. My eyes were still watering from the acrid cloud and the chemical composition of the haze did nothing good for my vocal cords.

The forward passenger entry door opened and the Chattanooga station manager led his passenger service agents bounding up the stairs like a S.W.A.T. team. It wasn't like the passengers were evacuating out the windows or anything. They were too stunned for that. The station manager was a glib fellow with a cadence of speech much like an auctioneer's. I'm not sure the passengers understood everything he said, but his authoritative demeanor had a calming effect on them. He was a multi-tasker: while babbling to the passengers, one hand on a microphone, his other hand directed me toward a fire marshal standing at the bottom of the stairs. The fire marshal was holding a stack of papers. It was just a wild guess, but I reckoned that somebody was going to have to pony up for our extravagant welcome. Fire trucks don't come cheap. With a reasonably steady hand, I affixed my signature to his documents. I had no idea what I was signing. It could have been the *Magna Carta*.

"You scared the shit out of us, son," the fire marshal said.

If he thought *he* had the shit scared out of him, he should have been sitting in *my* seat. He wasn't old enough to be my father, so I think he meant "son" as a gesture of affability. Or maybe "son" was just an abbreviation for "you son-of-a-gun." I smiled grimly or ruefully – I forget -- like someone who has been through hell to impress on the fire marshal what a challenge the whole ordeal had been.

It looked like I wasn't going to sleep in my own bed after all. On the other hand, I'd heard good things about Chattanooga. With luck, we might make it to the hotel before the bar closed down for the night. I intended to sip a Tennessee whiskey with Dave to celebrate our deliverance from being charbroiled by the Grim Reaper.

Tom Lee is the author of a light-hearted aviation book titled *There's a Turtle on the Runway*. It is available on Amazon.

Photo credit: Micha Klootwijk, Ivan Banchev, & feverpitched /123RF.com

Richard "Dick" Schafer

Beverly, Massachusetts
USAF School of Applied Ballistics
Master Sergeant, United States Air Force
C-5A Simulator
C-150, C-172, C-182, C-180,
PA-12, PA-20, PA-28, PA- 32,
IAI-1124 *Westwind*, AJ-1125 *Astra*
Lead Instructor, Flight Safety International

CHAPTER 11

SIX RULES

I'M WRITING THIS Reaper Buster story only because I believe that the statute of limitations on stupidity will protect me. I'll start with an accounting of how I got into close proximity with the Reaper, then, I'll reveal what happened when he tapped me on the shoulder.

I didn't start out wanting to be a pilot as a kid because I was convinced that God had destined me to be Sailing Master of a square-rigged clipper ship. I had my own copy of *Bowditch*, and I could name every sail, sheet, and line. Then my dad took me to the harbor at Gloucester, Massachusetts where there wasn't a sail in sight, just a fleet of smelly diesel fishing boats. I was devastated. I felt consigned to a life with my feet planted on earth until 1961 when I converted to a desire to be part of the new-fangled space program. At the time, I was an alternate for a Congressional appointment to the United States Air Force Academy. They never got to me, however, because the primary candidate ahead of me accepted a slot at the United States Naval Academy. I'm sorry to say that he subsequently died in Vietnam.

I was on the rebound when an Air Force recruiter promised me I could get into the space program. I defied my father by signing up for the delayed enlistment program right out of high school. The best thing about the deal was that I had all summer to enjoy a really cute girlfriend, my dad's baby blue '57 Ford convertible, and miles and miles of beaches from Boston to Maine. If ever there was a young man whose enlistment should *not* have been delayed, it was me. I was seventeen, my really cute girlfriend was fourteen, and I was on the verge of committing statutory you-know-what. Then the recruiter trashed my idyllic summer fantasy by calling me to say he had gotten me into missile school right away. I had ten days before the bus left for San Antonio, which turned out to be one of the hotter locations on the globe in July.

Indeed, I soon discovered that day-time temperatures at Lackland Air Force Base, Texas were hotter than the enchiladas they served in downtown San Antonio. I dodged heat prostration and headed up to Chanute Air Force Base, Illinois to attend Missile School. Soon after that, I went to Launch Control School in a place in Texas named after armadillos, I think. Check that: I just found out that Amarillo means "yellow" in Spanish. Finally, I showed up at Vandenberg Air Force Base, California, the only operational inter-continental ballistic missile (ICBM) base in the Strategic Air Command back then. So, at nineteen, I was a Combat Crew Qualified Engine Crew Chief on a nuclear-armed *Atlas* ICBM. Proving I didn't need "no stinkin' college," I was the tip of the spear defending the United States against the Great Red Menace. Four years later, I married the really cute girl. At about the same time, the Air Force declared the *Atlas* obsolete and replaced it with the solid-fueled *Minuteman*. Not to be cowed by my loss of prestige, I felt the need to seek adventure in Alaska.

I ended up at Elmendorf Air Force Base near the "Banana Belt" city of Anchorage where I almost immediately got hooked by a one-hour, ten-dollar introductory flying lesson. I got licenses and ratings as fast as possible – private, commercial, floats …. I flew out of Merrill Field, an "L-shaped" airport only about a mile from Elmendorf and about three miles from Anchorage International Airport. In addition to that, there were lots of other busy little airports, landing strips, and lakes all over the place. On a nice day, so many airplanes filled the skies over Anchorage that they looked like a swarm of flies buzzing over the town dump. There were a lot more airplanes overhead than there were cockpit radios or licensed pilots. To escape the beehive, I practiced my air work in one of Alaska's many isolated valleys where I could practice air work without seeing another airplane. I practiced stalls at a thousand feet above the ground to have enough room to recover.

Okay. That's enough about how I ended up solo in a Cessna a thousand feet above the Alaskan snow pack. Cue the Reaper.

Just as I rolled into sixty degrees of bank for a free-lance simulated attack on a moose down below, a huge object filled my windscreen. It was the biggest C-130 *Hercules* in the world. At least it was the *closest* C-130 *Hercules* in the world. Like the clipper ships and *Atlas* missiles in my past, I personally was about to become extinct real fast. I kept cranking in the bank, past the stall break, and went inverted, dropping like a rock. My little Cessna could have been sliced up by the huge four-bladed props powered by four roaring Alison T-56s like a lemon in a blender, but, somehow, it wasn't. Prop wash from the 125,000-pound C-130 travelling at 300 knots flipped me like a cork.

By the time I regained control of the Cessna at a hundred feet above the ground, the C-130 was … poof! … gone. I searched in every direction. All I could see was snow, rocks, and mountains in the distance. The crew was probably halfway to the Officers Club by then to talk about the grunts they'd para-dropped into snow banks in the interior somewhere and wondering whether they had smushed the Cessna down in the valley, the valley so low.

Inside my cockpit, my collection of charts had been completely reorganized by negative *G*s. What I could see of the exterior of the airplane looked fine – at least, I couldn't see any daylight through the tail. I sniffed the air. Although I couldn't detect anything out of the ordinary, I planned to conduct a more thorough diaper check when I got back to the barn.

I once read that ninety-nine per cent of good judgment comes from experience, and that ninety-nine percent of experience comes from bad judgment. After retiring from the Air Force, I put my "experience" to use for 20 years teaching at Flight Safety International. My subject, of all things, was aviation safety. I tried to pass along lessons learned from my blunders and the blunders of others. Sometimes I made *my* blunders sound like someone else's blunders in the interest of preserving self-respect. Along the way, I coined *"Schafer's Rules for Aviators."* Here they are:

1. Reality is ninety-nine per cent perception.
2. Predicaments are always easier to get *into* than *out* of. (This applies to more than just airports.)
3. There are three ways to do everything: the right way, the wrong way, and the Chief Pilot's way.
4. It's impossible to make anything totally foolproof because fools are so ingenious.
5. Never say "never" in aviation.
6. And never, *never* talk to a reporter.

These rules have helped me to avoid running afoul of the Grim Reaper again. Note: the day's not over, yet.

Photo courtesy of Dave Johnson

Dave "Fireball" Johnson

Roseau, Minnesota
Bemidji State University
Lieutenant, United States Navy
T-34, T-2A, F-9, F-11, F-8
Cessna 210

CHAPTER 12

FIREBALL

HOW I GOT my nickname is not a great mystery. In the space of about an hour one night, I smashed an F-8 *Crusader* to bits on the ramp of the *USS Shangri-La*, got hurled into the ocean, and was rescued by the crew of a destroyer. By all rights, my evening of adventure should have reduced me to fish chum. I certainly didn't escape that outcome by any skill or cunning on my part. The best chance the Grim Reaper ever had of bagging me started with a faulty angle of attack (AOA) system.

If you've longed to know more about AOA, this paragraph is for you. AOA is the angle formed by the mean aerodynamic chord of an airfoil – a wing -- and the relative wind. If you stick your hand out of a car window while driving at sixty miles an hour you can create a *low* AOA by holding your hand parallel to the road surface. You can generate a *high* AOA by tilting your fingers upwards, say, at 45 degrees above the horizon. It would be foolhardy to try this at 1,100 miles an hour, so engineers have provided most fighter aircraft with AOA lights, audio tones, and gauges to help pilots know, among other things, at what speed they're generating the maximum amount of lift versus drag. When landing on a carrier, if you fly your approach too much slower than this optimum AOA, you will stall, crash, and die.

If you fly too much *faster* than optimum AOA, you'll rip the tail hook off the plane, then crash and die. So, AOA matters.

On the night I almost burned, drowned, and got beat to death, my AOA indications looked good before takeoff, but they were worse than useless in the air. My *Crusader's* AOA system chose the moment I was catapulted off the ship to stop working. It resumed indicating a little later, so I pressed on, fully intending to fly close formation on my fearless leader during the sortie to make sure my AOA was indicating properly. Of course, I forgot. On with the mission!

I had just begun my final approach to land on the carrier when the AOA system failed again. I bravely pressed on. As if by magic, the AOA system began indicating a few seconds later, but the AOA was in disagreement with my airspeed indicator. AOA took precedence over airspeed indications. On I flew, too busy with other malfunctions to mention my airspeed/AOA woes to anyone.

I discovered that my automatic throttle wasn't working. That wasn't all. My wing lights chose the darkest night in a century to go on the blink, so I turned on my rotating beacon (non-standard) and opened my inflight-refueling door, which has a small light built into it to give the Landing Signals Officer (LSO) clues to my aircraft's position and attitude on final. My cockpit AOA indications showed exactly "on speed," but on the ship, the LSO's approach speed radar device was inoperative, so his only indications warned that I was fast. In fact, as we later discovered, I was exceptionally slow.

The next thing I knew, I was close to the *Shangri-La* and descending … fast. I selected full afterburner and pitched the nose up. Too late! I hit the round down of the ship and my *Crusader* broke up. The aircraft fuel tanks ruptured, and a huge fireball enveloped the back half of the fuselage which was in the middle of a somersault over the forward half of the airplane. The guys on the flight deck described it as the most spectacular explosion they had ever seen.

It was pretty extraordinary from my vantage point, too. At the time, I was flipping sideways across the Number Four Wire. Darkness in the cockpit and a raging inferno outside the cockpit convinced me that it was time to leave what remained of the aircraft.

I had to bend my head forward to clear the face curtain of the overhead ejection handles above my helmet. My greatest fear at that moment was that the seat would fire before I could straighten my posture and my neck would snap like a twig when the rocket blew my seat out of the cockpit. I got my head back against the head pad and tensed. The precaution prevented my neck from snapping, but it used up precious time, too. I heard a loud bang and the area below my feet lit up like a Roman candle. Figuring I had ejected, I grabbed for my Mae West flotation device toggles. Before I could pull them to inflate the vest, I blacked out.

I later discovered that remnants of the airplane had left the angled deck, rolled left, and entered the water upside down, taking me along for the ride. The ejection seat appeared to fire horizontally to the ocean's surface, but the camera that would have recorded the action was inoperative. (Surely, some mechanical component on the *Shangri-La* was in working order that night, but I can't think now what it was.)

Investigators determined that the tremendous jolt I felt occurred when my ejection seat and I slammed into the water. Only one cell of my Mae West flotation device inflated, so I should have drowned. Instead, I blacked out.

When I came to, I could see the carrier disappearing into the distant darkness. Desperate to keep my head above the water, I grabbed the leading edge of one of the demolished *Crusader's* wings, cutting my hand in the process. The weight of my soaking survival gear was too much for the buoyancy provided by a single cell of my Mae West. When the wing section began to sink under my weight, I knew I was in trouble. I heard voices shouting, "Grab the collar!" The voices belonged to crewmen on the plane guard destroyer that followed the carrier around to pick up guys like me.

I grabbed the rescue horse collar just before the wing and my parachute went underwater never to be seen again. On its way down, the parachute started pulling me under with it. Guys named Hendricks and Snodgrass couldn't release the parachute fasteners, so my submarine qualification trials were about to begin. Huge bubbles erupted from my mouth and nose as the parachute pulled me and the horse collar underwater. Thank God for Lieutenant Commander Furey who clambered down a net like Spider Man and, at the last second, sliced the parachute shroud lines that were dragging me under. My anti-exposure suit had ripped and was full of water, so it took five guys to haul me in.

As medics were cutting my gear off on a ward room table, it occurred to me that I may have been responsible for killing a lot of people on the carrier. A call to the *Shangri-La* confirmed that everyone on the carrier was okay. I passed out again.

The next day, a helicopter crew winched me up in a wire basket like a turkey in a basting pan to their hovering chopper. I was only halfway into the chopper when it lifted away for the short hop to the carrier. I felt like I was sliding out of the basket to tumble back into the ocean, but a guy with forearms like Popeye held on to me. Onboard the *Shangri-La*, I was placed to rest on a berth in sick bay.

When my commander Stolly Stollenwerck and Executive Officer Pete Easterling approached my bed, I figured that my flying days were over.

"Well, Dave, are you going to stay with us?"

I couldn't believe Stolly was giving me a choice.

"Yes, sir, if you'll let me," I said.

Like a father to a prodigal son, Stolly assured me that I still had a place in the squadron.

When I was finally cleared to fly 30 days later, I had a nagging concern that things might go wrong. I wasn't disappointed.

I couldn't get my first plane started.

The second airplane had a terminal hydraulic leak.

Finally, in an apparently airworthy airplane, I sat attached to the catapult, waiting to be tossed out over a body of water that had so recently attempted to murder me by drowning. The catapult failed to fire four times. It was almost as though the ocean had tasted me and didn't want any part of me. If it was baseball, I would have been back in the dugout after the third failed launch. Tension was mounting. I had never heard the expression "the fifth time's the charm," but it was. The next thing you know I was blasting out over the ocean, back in the saddle again flying a beautiful F-8 *Crusader*.

Later on I found out that a possible cause of my instrument malfunctions that dark, fiery night was an unreported accidental discharge of fire suppression foam into the cockpit. Fluids and electrical circuits, of course, don't mix well.

I also found out that my buddy Larry Durbin had been watching my recovery on a closed circuit monitoring screen in the Ready Room with Solly the night of the fireball. When they saw my aircraft slam into the round down of the carrier, causing exploding fuel tanks to light up the carrier deck as bright as day, Solly turned to Larry and said, "Get out the next-of-kin report. We just lost Dave."

Of course, they didn't lose Dave "Fireball" Johnson. I completed my Naval service successfully and largely without further conflagrations. I was never cocky about surviving the ordeal, but it was satisfying to imagine the Grim Reaper packing his unused marsh mellows back into his kit bag.

A full account of Dave Johnson's preternatural escape from the Reaper's wrath is included in Ron Knott's 2009 anthology *Supersonic Cowboys*.

Image credit: Don Hollway

Woodrow "Woodie" Bergeron

Blairsville, Georgia
Lieutenant Colonel, United States Air Force
F-4, A-10

CHAPTER 13

BOXER 22

"BOXER TWO-TWO, you're hit! Bail out!"

Pilot Captain Benjamin Danielson and Weapon Systems Officer (WSO) Woodrow "Woodie" Bergeron did what Boxer Flight Leader Major Joe Young told them to do: they punched out of their F-4 *Phantom* over Laos into a steep valley teeming with hundreds of enemy troops who wanted them dead. The only chance the downed airmen had of escaping the Reaper's wrath was a massive rescue effort.

It was the first flight together for Danielson, a native of Minnesota, and Bergeron, from Louisiana. They were members of the 558th Tactical Fighter Squadron "Phantom Knights" stationed at Cam Ranh Bay, South Vietnam. What a way to end their first sortie in combat as a team!

By the time they had put distance between themselves and their tell-tale parachutes, they realized that they were separated from one another by the Nam Ngo River at a choke point in the Ho Chi Minh Trail. Bergeron had suffered a broken nose and a gash in his head when the wind blast tore off his helmet during ejection. His wounds were the least of his worries, however, as he quickly discovered that he and his pilot had landed in the middle of a region near Ban Pha Nop village that was crawling with North Vietnamese soldiers.

Photo credit: Don Hollway

Captain Benjamin Danielson

Air Force helicopters made several attempts to extract Danielson and Bergeron, but intense anti-aircraft fire forced them to retreat. It didn't take a William Tell or a Daniel Boone to hit a hovering helicopter, and North Vietnamese gunners of all skill levels were effective in driving away all rescue attempts. Seven helicopters were grounded by battle damage at day's end. The failed extraction attempts took an emotional toll on Danielson and Bergeron, because the helicopters had probed as close as 30 feet from their positions. So close, yet, so far.

By sundown, a total of 90 American fighter aircraft, including the A-1 *Sandy*, F-100 *Super Sabre*, F-105 *Thunderchief*, A-6 *Intruder*, and F-4 *Phantom,* had dropped more than 300 bombs and rockets on enemy positions in the Nam Ngo Valley, but the enemy guns and artillery were still too formidable for helicopters to get in. Maintenance crews at the special operations search and rescue headquarters at Nakhon Phanom, Thailand, worked all night to produce airworthy helicopters for resumption of rescue efforts the following day, December 6, 1969.

Danielson and Bergeron dug in for the night and hoped that roaming patrols of enemy soldiers would fire into any clump of bushes except the ones in which they had chosen to hide.

First Lieutenant Woody Bergeron

On the following morning, the North Vietnamese found Danielson and killed him immediately. Powerless to intervene, Bergeron watched from his hiding spot across the river. He faced two likely outcomes, and neither of them involved being taken prisoner. There was a slim chance of rescue, but, much more likely, he would die in a hail of bullets like his friend. Nevertheless, Bergeron took heart in the fact that, although a steady stream of enemy firepower was streaming down the Ho Chi Minh Trail, Nakhon Phanom was only 65 miles away.

General George S. Brown, Seventh Air Force commander, committed every resource available to the effort to extract Bergeron. Every pilot in Vietnam, Laos, and Thailand knew the Boxer Two-Two call sign by now, and they were eager to get Bergeron out.

Throughout the day, Bergeron used his survival radio to call in air strikes each time another band of enemy soldiers got too close to his hiding place. The proximity of exploding

2,000-pound bombs dropped to silence enemy cannons and guns was so near that the concussions actually lifted Bergeron off the ground a couple of inches. Levitation had never felt so good. The cacophony of explosions and gun fire reverberated all day. Some of the blasts temporarily deafened Bergeron. One friendly strafing pass missed him by only a foot. A tear gas bomblet actually bounced off his chest. The first whiff of the gas made him involuntarily urinate and vomit, compounding the mental and psychological toll on him.

Bergeron was close enough to a shallow stretch of the Nam Ngo used by North Vietnamese convoys as a river crossing that he learned the flashlight signals that enemy soldiers were using to start and stop the winch that powered trucks and mobile guns from shore to shore. When a platoon of hostile infantrymen approached Bergeron's hiding place by wading into the river, Bergeron called in a strafing pass. He watched in awe as a *Sandy's* 20-millimeter bullets shredded his attackers.

Near the end of the second day, the North Vietnamese had a general idea of where Bergeron was hiding. As the American planes retired for the night, enemy patrols started narrowing their search. They tossed a tear gas bomblet into a tangle of bushes and machine-gunned it in the dark. All they found, as they searched without a flashlight, was Bergeron's survival gear. Bergeron, weak and hungry, had moved to new cover down the river, losing his .38-caliber revolver in the process. Night time brought on cold, hunger, and hallucinations. Bergeron didn't have much left in the tank. Something had to give or the Reaper would claim his prize.

The following morning, at dawn of Day Three, a *Sandy* pilot radioed to ask Bergeron the name of his best friend. It was one of Bergeron's authentication questions, and, even in his exhausted state, he knew the answer.

"Weisdorfer," Bergeron croaked.

The pilot radioed back that he didn't have time to check, but, echoing the Smucker's tag line, he decided that, "with a name like that, it has to be you."

A gaggle of A-1s set up counter-rotating wheel patterns and kept constant pressure on the enemy by laying down smoke, hitting targets of opportunity, and strafing any of the mass of 1,000 infantrymen that had formed up for a frontal assault on Bergeron's hideout.

Still taking enemy fire, a *Jolly Green Giant* helicopter appeared out of the smoke and lowered a bullet-shaped rescue hoist equipped with spring-loaded flip-out seats. The penetrator device splashed into the river not four feet from Bergeron's hiding spot. One of the helicopter's machine gunners raked hostile troops across the river. The other door gunner fired a stream of machine gun fire into more than 20 soldiers charging to within 30 feet of Bergeron, who was scrambling madly to mount the penetrator and secure himself in the harness.

Helicopter crewmen hoisted Bergeron up toward the open helicopter door and tugged him inside like a sack of turnips. The aircraft commander wasted no time; he used maximum power to get out of the little province of hell beside the Nam Ngo River.

The rescue of Boxer 22 was the largest search and rescue mission of the Vietnam War. A total of 336 sorties were flown by American aircraft. They expended 1,463 bombs and pods of rockets over the course of three days. A-1s alone flew 242 sorties; HH-3 and HH-53 helicopters, over 40. Five A-1s were damaged and eventually repaired, but five of the battle-damaged helicopters never flew again.

In 2003 Benjamin Danielson's dog tags and human remains were located near the Nam Ngo River in Laos. Captain Danielson was laid to rest in his hometown -- Kenyon, Minnesota -- by his son, United States Navy Lieutenant Commander Brian Danielson. (Brian had not reached the age of two years when his father was shot down.)

"Woody" Bergeron was awarded a Silver Star for his valiant efforts to report intelligence about the massing of enemy forces on the banks of the Nam Ngo River during his two days of perilous evasion. Having narrowly survived his clash with the Grim Reaper, he continued to serve in the United States Air Force as an A-10 *Thunderbolt* pilot. He retired in 1987 having reached the rank of Lieutenant Colonel.

For an in-depth account of this remarkable rescue operation, read military historian Don Hollway's articles on his web site at donhollway.com/boxer22, on history.net, and in *Vietnam Magazine*.

Hollway, Don. "Saving Boxer 22." Vietnam Magazine, 2018.

LaPointe, Robert. *All for One: The Rescue of Boxer 22*. Northern PJ Press, 2002.

Malayney, Norman. "A Summary of December 1969 Events for Boxer 22." www.12tfw/boxer22.

Tilford, Earl H. *Search and Rescue: The USAF in Southeast Asia*. Center for Air Force History, 1980.

PBY *Catalina* photo credit: Andrew Oxley & David Wingate/123RF.com

Dick Whitfield
United States Navy
Lieutenant JG
TBM *Avenger*

CHAPTER 14

LOST

SOMETIMES the Grim Reaper bungles a kill as though it simply wasn't time yet. A prime example is this story about an Okinawa-based TBM *Avenger* pilot named Dick Whitfield, a feisty man who had no intention of filling the Grim Reaper's quota. The week had started out rough.

Japanese bombers sprang a suicide raid on Yontan, Okinawa. (The Emperor's minions invented as many ways to commit suicide as the French had varieties of cheese.) They crammed heavily armed soldiers into seven bombers, hoping to plant them on the American runway at Yontan. (Volunteers for suicide missions were scarce, so the seven pilots chosen didn't have to be the best sticks in the Land of the Rising Sun.) All Japanese soldiers who survived the landings were supposed to stream from the bombers to spread across the ramp, whooping like maniacs, tossing hand grenades every which way, and firing indiscriminately at everything that moved ... or didn't move. Execution of the plan was less than dazzling.

American Navy anti-aircraft guns brought down three of the seven bombers before they reached the island. The intruders were flying so low that anti-aircraft gunners were firing almost horizontally, at angles depressed enough to make friendly fire a concern. Three more Japanese bombers were destroyed in the air above the runway. That left one bomber that got through to crash land on the runway.

More than 60 Japanese soldiers dispersed across the ramp like fire ants emerging from an ant hill. They tossed hand grenades at airplanes and fired machine guns at Marines guarding the airfield. They succeeded in blowing up over 70,000 gallons of aviation fuel, damaging 40 aircraft, and killing two Marines. At dawn, Marines counted 69 dead Japanese suicide attackers.

Neither Dick Whitfield nor any of his fellow TBM *Avenger* pilots were seriously injured in the raid, and, within hours, Whitfield was back on anti-submarine patrol in a single-engine TBM *Avenger*. His crew included a turret gunner and a multi-tasker who wore three hats – radioman, ventral gunner, and bombardier. In addition to bombs, torpedoes, and depth charges, the *Avenger* was armed with a .30-caliber nose gun, a rear-mounted .50-caliber gun mounted on top of the fuselage, and a .30-caliber tail gun mounted under the horizontal stabilizer. Searching for Japanese submarines was monotonous work because the Pacific Ocean was such a huge body of water that trying to find a submarine was like looking for a missing pearl on a beach. The chances of spotting an enemy submarine on the surface were remote. Whitfield's mind-numbing patrol was much less likely be interrupted by an opportunity to attack a submarine than by being attacked by a terrifying swarm of Japanese *Zero* fighters. After hours of fruitless searching, it was time for Whitfield to recover to Okinawa.

He had been flying over a broken deck of clouds for so long that he didn't know exactly where he was. He was what pilots euphemistically call "temporarily disoriented." The consequences of being temporarily disoriented over the Pacific Ocean were serious. Every Navy pilot who reported for duty in the Pacific quickly learned how easy it was to get lost over the world's largest ocean, never to be found. Being lost over the Pacific wasn't like being lost an Interstate highway, where the worst that can happen is that you discover that you're going the wrong way, so you find an exit, pull over to buy a tank of gas and a candy bar, and set off in the reverse direction. Over the Pacific, a course error of only three or four degrees was enough to make a pilot miss his landfall. He could fly all day and never see an island. Whitfield radioed Ground Control and requested a bearing to home base.

The difference between the bearing *to* the air base and the bearing *from* the air base was 180 degrees. Apparently, the A Team wasn't on duty that day, because the ground controller gave Whitfield the bearing *from* the airdrome, so Whitfield toodled off in exactly the wrong direction. A more rigid standard of professional curiosity might have caught the error, but Whitfield and his crew were bored senseless after a long patrol and all they could think about was tearing into a good can of spam and a beer. Thus, the stalwart crew flew blithely on top of a white blanket of clouds *away* from their desired destination.

Well past the time when Whitfield should have reached the airfield, the PBY's low fuel state was jangling the nerves of the crew. Through a break in the clouds, they spotted a military airport, and Whitfield jubilantly dove through the "sucker hole" for a visual approach. A closer inspection dispelled his joy because every single airplane on the ramp had Japanese markings. Whitfield didn't know where he was, but it certainly wasn't Okinawa. He turned around as unobtrusively as possible to backtrack.

Luckily, no Japanese fighters scrambled to complicate Whitfield's agonizing retreat as he retraced his flight path. The steady march of the fuel quantity gauge toward empty reminded Whitfield of his stupidity. Admitting it was a tiresome exercise, but time passed quickly, and, much sooner than he wanted, the engine sputtered and shut down for lack of fuel. Although he didn't know it at the time, he was more than a hundred miles from Okinawa. All he knew was that he was conducting a deathly quiet descent toward a water landing called, cacophonously, "ditching."

Whitfield's ditching maneuver couldn't have been smoother. After impact, the plane floated for a time because of the buoyancy of empty fuel tanks. As the fuselage slowly slipped beneath the waves, Whitfield directed evacuation of the aircraft. In an effort to make up for the mistake that put them in the water in the first place, Whitfield made certain that he stocked the two survival rafts with every item that might be of use during their pending survival challenge.

Shortly after the TBM had sunk into the ocean, Whitfield's crew rigged blue sails over their rafts and began to sail toward somewhere. They had little food or water, so they were keenly hopeful that they would be found by Americans. They were even more intensely hopeful that they *wouldn't* be found by a Japanese patrol.

During the four miserable days that followed, Whitfield's small band survived a tropical storm, multiple disappointments, and moments of terror. They shot flares to capture the attention of passing American airplanes. They hid from Japanese airplanes by lowering their sails to camouflage their rafts. If a plane turned out to be American, Whitfield's crew would flap the sails like lunatics, hoping to be seen. They got lucky on the fifth day. As a PBY *Catalina* seaplane passed overhead, the PBY crew detected a mirror flash from one of the rafts. The PBY was carrying a dignitary who had a schedule to keep, so the PBY continued flying westward. Whitfield and his crew were discouraged. They had no way of knowing that the passing PBY had radioed their position to another seaplane which was on its way to rescue them. They had almost given in to hunger, thirst, fatigue, and sea sickness when the second American *Catalina* descended to land hard on the turbulent surface of the sea.

The seaplane pilot skillfully maneuvered the *Catalina* so Whitfield and his crew could clamber aboard. As a defiant act reminiscent of James Bowie at the Alamo, Whitfield slashed both rafts with his survival knife so the enemy couldn't benefit from them in any way.

"I wouldn't have done that," the *Catalina* pilot said. "We've sprung several plates in our bow and this bucket of bolts might sink."

The plane didn't sink, but it was damaged enough that it couldn't take off in the rough seas. The only solution was to taxi the 100 miles back to Okinawa. Making way at eight knots over the water, the *Catalina* was a sitting duck for Japanese patrols. The Americans were in luck; twelve hours later, the damaged plane reached Okinawa.

Whitfield's squadron mates were a rowdy bunch. When they heard about his rescue, they prepared an elaborate prank. They removed his cot and all of his possessions from his bedroom and hid them. The conspirators were disappointed when Whitfield was taken directly to a hospital and didn't show up at the squadron for a few days. While his pals impatiently awaited his return, Whitfield faced medical challenges. He had lost weight and was suffering from sun burn. He also had developed hemorrhoids while floating in the life raft, so a doctor performed corrective surgery. While he was at it, he performed another procedure at no extra charge.

"I circumcised you while I was in the neighborhood," was the way the doctor put it to the slightly modified and thoroughly astonished aviator when he had emerged from the fog of anesthesia. On account of his painful derriere and his swollen "crotchal" area, Whitfield couldn't lie on his stomach *or* his back, so sleep was elusive for many days. Finally, when anal and genital swelling had abated, he returned to his squadron and an empty tent.

"Welcome home!" his fellow pilots bellowed. "We had a wake for you and drank all your whiskey. We also gave your bed to a new guy, gave your clothes to some Okinawans, and sent your love letters to your mother!"

"I know what it feels like to be dead," Whitfield said.

When his buddies had tired of their horseplay, they put his cot back together, returned all his possessions, and had a party at which they actually *did* drink all of Whitfield's whiskey while he regaled them with the details of his rescue and circumcision.

"I feel like less of a man," Whitfield complained. His fellow pilots would have none of his self-pity.

"I don't want to hear about your cock getting cut off," one buddy said. "Tell us about your four days in the raft."

Like a fisherman catching and releasing a trout out of season, the Reaper had tossed Whitfield back, perhaps, to have a go at him at a later date.

Hynes, Samuel. *Flights of Passage.* Pocket Books, 1988.

Photo credit: Boeing/United States Air Force

B-52 *Stratofortress*

CHAPTER 15

SHEAR

AMERICA'S FRONT-LINE bomber, the 580,000-pound B-52 *Stratofortress,* without a vertical stabilizer looks as unstable as a pencil with two popsicle sticks pasted on to it. Almost no one would think that it could fly that way, but, on January 10, 1964, it did – for almost six hours. A bit of history is in order.

The Cold War was a lot like a chess match. The Soviet Union's rustic General Secretary Nikita Khrushchev built hundreds of intercontinental ballistic missiles with nukes on their tips. Displaying a fondness for bluntness over statesmanship, he threatened to bury the United States. His bluster induced paranoia in the Western world for years. He shocked the United Nations assembly by theatrically hammering a table with a shoe as if tenderizing a flank steak. His antics disconcerted the European and American public because their memories of what nukes could do (as in Hiroshima and Nagasaki) were fresh in their minds, and Khrushchev looked like just the guy to make it happen.

Air raid sirens were installed across the Fruited Plain. Home bomb shelters were dug under lawns all over America. Not only could a bomb shelter prolong the lives of loved ones for up to two weeks after Armageddon, it was a perfect place to store canned goods. In the United States, a generation of school kids practiced sheltering beneath their desks. They were only vaguely aware of why they were hunkering down under desks among huge gobs of chewing gum that pockmarked their makeshift bomb shelters. Kids generally didn't object to the nuclear shelter exercises because every minute spent under a desk was a minute not spent on multiplication tables.

Over time, the United States countered the Russians by putting nuclear warheads into silos, onto railroad cars, in submarines, and aboard bombers so the Reds wouldn't get any wild ideas. There was a big problem with the 1950's fleet of 384 B-36 *Peacemakers* that made up America's defensive shield. Not only did a B-36 have six engines pointing backwards, it couldn't cruise any faster than 400 mph on a good day and it couldn't extend its 10,000-mile range by in-flight refueling. America needed faster new bombers and a way to extend their operating range.

The Soviets weren't just lounging around drinking straight Baikal vodka, either. First, they upgraded their fleet by producing the Tu-4 *Bull*, a copy of the American B-29 *Superfortress*. Starting in 1954, the Russians built 1,500 medium range Tu-16 *Badgers* and 100 M-4 *Bisons*. Then, two years later, they introduced the first of 500 Tu-95 *Bears*. In 1962 they began to phase in over 300 Tu-22 *Blinders* capable of a top speed of 1,300 mph. Tu-22 *Backfires* subsequently filled the Russian's perceived need for a medium-range bomber.

To counter this threat, the United States built a total of 2,032 B-47 *Stratojets*, sexy machines with six jets on the wings that lifted the B-47 to 35,000 feet and propelled it to over 600 mph with a payload of 25,000 pounds. Manned by a crew of three, it could fly far into Russia, but without a guarantee that it would have enough gas to get from the target back home (presuming there would be a home to get back to). The B-47 became America's first intercontinental bomber capable of in-flight refueling.

Piston-powered KC-97 *Stratotankers* were the only air-refueling tankers available to the United States at the time. Starting in 1950, the Air Force had acquired more than 800 KC-97s, a type of aircraft with serious limitations. Its operational altitude was well below the B-47's, and it was so slow that, as B-52 *Stratofortresses* came into the inventory, they had to lower flaps and aft landing gear in order to in-flight refuel from the slow KC-97s.

Then, in 1956, along came the first of 800 four-engine, jet-powered air-refueling KC-135 *Stratotankers*. That same year, the Air Force began replacing B-47 squadrons with much larger B-52 *Superfortresses*. Over 740 B-52s were delivered. The eight-engine bomber, generally manned by a crew of five, had a hefty maximum takeoff gross weight of 588,000 pounds. It could reach an altitude of 50,000 feet when loaded to less than capacity, reach a speed of 650 mph, and fly 10,000 miles without in-flight refueling.

Soon after that, the Air Force introduced the first American supersonic bomber, the B-58 *Hustler*. Only 118 were built. The *Hustler's* maximum speed was 1,319 mph (Mach 2) and its service ceiling was over 63,000 feet. The *Hustler* set 19 world speed records, some of them held by singer John Denver's father, Air Force Lt. Col. Henry J. Deutschendorf, Sr. Before long, the *Hustler's* role diminished and the B-52 *Stratofortress* became the primary Air Force bomber for more than 50 years.

Meanwhile the crafty rascals in Moscow had developed a sophisticated and capable air defense system. It quickly became clear to American planners that high altitude operations by B-52s would be vulnerable to the well-coordinated Russian network of surface-to-air missiles. It appeared that the only way to get past all those radars and missiles and guns was going in fast down on the deck. Low level ingress training began in earnest.

Unfortunately, the B-52 wasn't designed for punishing low level flying in thermals and shears. Structural fatigue was eight times greater during a low level ingress at 300 feet above the ground than at six to eight miles above the earth. B-52 vertical stabilizers ("tails" for non-flyers) began falling off. Half a dozen B-52s crashed because of vertical stabilizer failure events in Canada, New Mexico, Maine, and Maryland.

Boeing borrowed a B-52 from the Air Force to conduct low-altitude stress tests. Boeing packed the aircraft with 20 accelerometers and over 200 sensors and, on January 10, 1964, pilot-in-command Chuck Fisher and pilot Richard Curry flew a test track east of the Rockies at 500 feet above the ground on autopilot. Speed ranged from 280 to 400 knots.

While paralleling the Rocky Mountains, Curry's engineers and technicians detected excessive loads on the tail because of increasing turbulence. Curry attempted to climb out of the turbulence. Passing through 14,300 feet near Mora, New Mexico, a violent shear of wind hit the B-52 with a series of explosive gusts. Navigator James Pitman was thrown across the width of the fuselage over the navigator's table and against the left interior of the airplane.

Fisher assumed control of the unstable aircraft and shoved in full left rudder, full left ailerons, and full aft yoke. The airplane lunged left then reversed violently to the right. Fisher told the other three crewmembers to prepare to bail out. The aircraft was vibrating at a high frequency like a tuning fork. Rudder was unresponsive.

At last, Fisher regained control of the aircraft. Only when he had flown back toward Boeing at Wichita and an F-100 *Super Sabre* had visually inspected the exterior of the bomber did Fisher know that more than eighty per cent of the B-52's vertical stabilizer was gone.

Engineers in an Emergency Control Center (ECC) at Boeing at Wichita advised the crew to transfer fuel to maintain a suitably forward center of gravity and to lower the aft gear to improve longitudinal stability. The crew canceled plans to bail out. The ECC coordinated with a B-52 on a routine training flight to evaluate various landing configurations so they could advise Fisher how to configure the damaged aircraft for landing. A KC-135 full of engineers got airborne and escorted the damaged bomber. It also served as an airborne command center.

Fisher was unable to land at the Boeing facility near Wichita because of adverse winds, so he diverted to Blytheville Air Force Base, Arkansas. His target speed on final approach was 200 knots. After retarding throttles to idle just before touchdown, the aircraft started to yaw left. Fisher hastily put the airplane on the ground, deployed the drag chute at 130 knots, and got the beast stopped on the runway. The flight had lasted six-hours, most of it without the largest vertical stabilizer in the world.

Instrument data revealed that gust loads of greater than 80 knots had been responsible for the vertical stabilizer failure and separation. Engineers subsequently strengthened the empennage section of B-52s. Tail number 61-0023 was repaired and returned to service where it logged 44 years of flying until being decommissioned on July 24, 2008. Fittingly, it was the first B-52H to be placed in the "Boneyard" aircraft storage facility at Davis-Monthan Air Force Base, Arizona.

The Reaper must have been sorely disappointed. What did a Prince of Doom have to do to bring an airplane down anymore? On that cold January day in 1964, a combination of pilot skill and engineering expertise foiled the Reaper's diabolical scheme.

Bukharin, Oleg, Pavel L. Podvig and Frank von Hippel. *Russian Strategic Nuclear Forces*. MIT Press, 2004.

Eden, Paul, ed. *Encyclopedia of Modern Military Aircraft*. Amber Books, 2004.

Gordon, Yefim and Peter Davidson. *Tupolev Tu-95 Bear*. North Branch, Minnesota Specialty Press, 2006.

Mizokami,Kyle. "The Time a B-52 Landed Without a Tail Fin." Popular Mechanics, August 1, 2017.

Wilson, Stewart. *Combat Aircraft since 1945*. Aerospace Publications, 2000.

Photo credit: icholakov01 & fotofritz/depositphotos.com

Odell Dobson

North Carolina
Staff Sergeant, USAAF
B-24 *Liberator*

CHAPTER 16

MORALE

THE LIVES OF AIRMEN in World War II often ended quickly and violently at the cruel hands of the Grim Reaper. Some of them, having outfoxed the Reaper during an air battle, confronted him on the ground as they suffered serious injuries, evaded capture, attempted to escape, endured abuse by captors, and persisted despite hunger, illness, and pain. A strong will to live, trust in colleagues, and a splash of audacity were qualities that improved a downed airman's chances of foiling the Reaper. A man with those qualities in spades was Odell Dobson, a waist gunner on a B-24 *Liberator*, a heavy bomber that carried six gunners. Dobson was overhead Hanover, Germany on September 11, 1944 when he became one of more than 20,000 B-24 crewmen to be shot down in World War II.

Considering that the objective of his missions was to bomb the crap out of Germany, it was an irony that one of Dobson's forebears had come to America as a Hessian mercenary. Dobson was a hustler, though, and he didn't let his ancestry stand in the way of his desire to do whatever it took to smack Hitler in the mouth. Dobson helped his impoverished family by lying about his age to land a job. (If women were prone to fib about being younger than they really were, boys at the time were notorious for doing the opposite.) Dobson's insatiable reading about World War I primed him to become a military man. He fulfilled his destiny in a circuitous, sometimes amusing, fashion.

He volunteered under-age for the Army Air Corps by scamming a permission note from his mother. He bulked up by ten pounds for pilot training by gorging on bananas and milk. He was as sick as a dog and he almost blew a bladder gasket, but he made weight. Following that round of monkey business, he washed out of pilot training.

He decided that he wanted to be a gunner even though he was six feet, two inches, seven inches above the five feet, six-inch height restriction. He solved the problem by forging a medic's signature. Dobson in a ball turret made a sardine can look spacious. He finagled an assignment to be a waist gunner, a position that afforded more head room. He barely passed gunnery school in Harlingen, Texas in time to meet up with his crew to fly a B-24 called *Rudd's Ruffians* to join the newly-formed 578th Bomb Squadron at Wendling, England. In short, Dobson had joined an organization full of men who took an oath to refrain from lying, cheating, or stealing by ... lying, cheating, and stealing. His roguish nature made him a perfect fit.

On one of Dobson's early missions over Germany, his plane was badly shot up inbound to the target. As a precaution, the navigator plotted a course for neutral Sweden, but aircraft commander Lt. C.A. Rudd wasn't interested. He flew the damaged plane onward to bomb the harbor at Kiel, suffering more anti-aircraft damage over the target. Rudd turned his battered *Liberator* toward home. One place *Rudd's Ruffians* should have avoided overflying at all costs was Heligoland Island. Anti-aircraft guns were as densely-packed on Heligoland as a pack of cigarettes. Of course, Rudd flew directly overhead the island. The penalty for Rudd's lack of navigational prowess was to get shot up again. Like a chunk of Swiss cheese with wings, *Rudd's*

Ruffians limped on toward Scotland, losing altitude all the way. Rudd safely landed the B-24 at an emergency field in Scotland. The *Liberator* was totaled and never flew again.

The squadron commander offered a deal that Rudd and his crew couldn't refuse. The prize was *Ford's Folly,* the first B-24 built by the Ford Motor Company of America. *Ford's Folly* was little more than a flyable wreck, having already flown 79 missions on more raids than any other bomber in Europe. The commander promised that if Rudd flew Dobson and his mates in *Ford's Folly* up to 100 missions, they could fly the *Liberator* back to the United States on a War Bond tour. Who could resist the promise of glory and girls? Dobson's buddies on *Ford's Folly* refused to count their next mission as Number 13 for persuasive reasons of a superstitious nature, so they called it "Mission 12A." Radio Operator Roger Clapp poured cold water on the plan, saying, "This is Mission Thirteen, boys, and we're going down."

Their thirteenth mission against Hanover didn't begin well. The tail gunner had no power to his guns, the nose gunner's sights wouldn't light up, the right waist gunner had to repair his gun with parachute cord, and left waist gunner Dobson, who had just repaired the ammunition feed chute of his machine guns with wire, accidentally knocked off his front gunsight. The middle portion of the mission didn't go any better. A swarm of Messerschmitt Me-109s attacked without mercy. The last moments of the war effort of *Ford's Folly* were frantic. They lost both engines on the right wing. The right waist gunner shot down two Me-109s. Dobson was dueling with an Me-109 on the left side of the damaged bomber when the fighter's stream of bullets blew up Dobson's gun. Shrapnel tore into Dobson's legs and chest. One piece of metal imbedded itself in Dobson's head, right between the eyes. Dobson was knocked down and blinded.

Luftwaffe fighters continued to rip *Ford's Folly* apart with machine gun fire. Hoganson, the right waist gunner, was the only gunner still able to shoot. He was knocked to the deck twice by German bullets, and both times he climbed back up to continue firing at the attackers. He shot down another Me-109. When he was shot a third time, Hoganson didn't get up again.

Ford's Folly entered a spin. Despite centrifugal forces, Dobson clipped on his parachute and fell free feet-first through a camera hatch. Dobson's chest was a mass of jelly, his legs were badly injured, and fragments in his face obstructed the vision in his left eye. He landed in a field near Treis, Germany. He had heard about irate German civilians hanging bomber crewmen from telephone poles and lighting their bodies on fire. Later, as he was being beaten and forced to walk on shattered legs, there were times when lynching and immolation sounded pretty good.

Without anesthesia of any kind and while strapped to a table, Dobson submitted to the probing, slicing, and extraction of metal fragments from his body by a disagreeable German corporal wielding a sharp scalpel. A nurse attempted to console Dobson by holding his hand. Satisfied in general with his work, the amateur surgeon gave up trying to wrestle out a piece of metal imbedded in Dobson's forehead.

"*Ve* finish," he said.

Dobson was transferred by train to a hospital in Giessen. Escaping was never far from Dobson's mind, but opportunities were fleeting. When a German commander ordered the immediate execution of escaping prisoners, Dobson lost his enthusiasm for breaking out. He subsisted on coffee made from acorns. Prison bread was mixed with saw dust to give it mass. Butter was extracted from tree sap. After a series of interrogations, he was transferred to a hospital run by captured British medical personnel. During Dobson's slow return to health, he met several prisoners who were worse off than he was.

Smitty, for example had peeked over the rim of his fox hole in time for a German bomb to implant a four-inch piece of shrapnel into his face just below his right eye. The razor-sharp shrapnel had torn out his cheekbone, obliterated the roof of his mouth, torn out part of his jaw, sliced off a portion of his tongue, perforated the bottom of his mouth, and stuck out of his neck, but he was still alive to mumble about it.

Jock was a Scots paratrooper renowned for his dramatic stories of sabotage against the German rail system. According to his accounts, he had hopped onto slowly-moving trains to uncouple as many box cars as possible. Then, still unobserved, he had left the train and walked back to each car at his leisure to set it ablaze. It was doubtful that his present diminished condition would permit any train-hopping in the future.

One British soldier had been shot in the right eye by a rifle bullet that traveled through his cranium and exploded out of the back of his head. Of course, he missed his right eye profoundly, but, within a month, he was playing poker with Dobson and winning more than he lost.

On the railway to Meiningen, Dobson's train suddenly stopped. All the German soldiers on board scampered off to get low in ditches, leaving the patients to bear the brunt of Allied bombs. Formations of American B-17s flew low over Dobson's head, so low he could see bombs stacked in their bomb bays. Dobson watched in wonder as he contemplated the injustice of having survived so much hardship only to be blown to bits by a bomb made in his own country and dropped on him by a brother-in-arms. Dobson lived through the experience. Short of snuffing out Dobson's life, the best the Reaper could do was to temporarily deafen him.

Stalag IV, near Keilheide, a German town on the Polish border, was Dobson's new home. Eight thousand American enlisted men and two thousand British airmen were imprisoned there. One of Dobson's best friends was a navigator who had studied Russian at the University of Texas. The Germans treated Russian prisoners atrociously, bringing them into Stalag IV every day to perform filthy tasks like emptying latrines. One day, carrying out a secret plan, the Texan barked orders in Russian at more than 20 Russians. He lined them in threes and marched them into the compound without interference by German guards. The plan worked flawlessly. The Russians were parceled out among the American prisoners to receive a wash, a shave, and a haircut. They were outfitted in American uniforms and integrated into the mass of ten thousand prisoners.

The poop hit the fan at roll call when the Germans conducted three head counts to confirm that they had 24 too many prisoners. The prisoners stymied every effort by the Germans to solve the riddle. Dobson risked punishment or death along with hundreds of other American prisoners by confounding German efforts to separate the sheep from the goats. The final step was a giant snowball fight that convinced the Germans to end two days of counting efforts. Dobson realized that participating in the ruse hadn't influenced the war, but it had probably saved the lives of two dozen Russians.

In February of 1945, the 8,000 American prisoners were forced to begin a march of what was promised to be four days to cover 100 miles west toward Stargard. Vicious dogs and a large contingent of guards kept prisoners moving through bitterly cold weather. At the end of four days, the Germans pressed the huge column of American airmen on, eventually for more than 80 days!

Prisoners were issued three potatoes and a piece of black bread on most days. Dobson foraged for food from roadside forests whenever the huge column of men stopped marching for the night. When snowfall was light, Dobson helped steal tractor parts from farms to hamper German food production. He urinated on piles of grain, anything to complicate the lives of his captors. During heavy snows, the prisoners trudged on despite illness, shivering, and frostbite. They paused at a French prisoner-of-war camp where the prisoners lived in brick buildings and enjoyed relatively ample food rations. Dobson begged for a little food for his men, but the French refused his request.

When American fighters flew low overhead, Dobson waved a makeshift American flag so the fighters wouldn't strafe the prisoners. Well into their second month of marching on the edge of death, Dobson and his fellow prisoners approached a column of 12,000 Royal Air Force airmen. Unfortunately for the British column, eight RAF *Typhoons* failed to recognize their countrymen. The strafing killed sixty men and wounded forty others.

Outside the town of Büchen, Dobson's immense column of surviving marchers bivouacked at a large farm. Dobson was too weak to cause mischief and too weak to forage for food. The scrappy waist gunner had reached his limit. Whatever punishment the Germans would impose, he knew that he had taken his last step. The Reaper had whittled away at Dobson's determination for three months of near starvation and forced marching, and, now, by dawn's early light, the Reaper hoped to end Dobson's life.

On that following morning, May 2, 1945, Dobson rose stiffly from his place in a field and found a quiet place in a barn to eat his last potato and smoke his last cigarette. Several prisoners burst through the barn door celebrating. Dobson followed them outside and climbed a massive manure heap to get a better view. A British lieutenant standing on a jeep told the assembled prisoners that they were officially liberated. Prisoners disarmed their guards as instructed and began moving toward Büchen.

Almost 8,000 Americans, Dobson among them, escaped the Reaper's grasp in a flash. Dobson's face, chest, and legs were scarred for life. He was destined to bear fragments of steel and aluminum in his face until his death. Dobson had found the war he had dreamed of as a boy, and he had emerged from it as a man, too wise to dream, but still as feisty as when he had started. Odell Dobson was free.

Lewis, Bruce. *Four Men Went To War*. St. Martin's Press, 1978.

John "Slick" Furneaux

Key Largo, Florida
Western Washington State College
Captain, United States Air Force
F-4, F-15
B-737, DC-9, A-321
Air Florida, US Airways, Eastern Airlines,
Vice President – Flight Operations

CHAPTER 17

BLUE

THE REAPER's a wily scoundrel who knows that, on a sunny day, the ocean is the same color as the sky. Blue.

Not long after my transition from the F-4 *Phantom* to the F-15 *Eagle* at Bitburg Air Base, Germany, I was sent to Langley Air Force Base, Virginia temporarily to maintain F-15 proficiency with the 94th Fighter Squadron, Eddie Rickenbacker's World War I "Hat-in-the-Ring Squadron." The trans-Atlantic shuffle was necessary because Bitburg's 36th Fighter Wing had taken delivery of only three of its eventual complement of seventy-two F-15s.

Our mission on the beautiful, cloudless day in question involved launching four *Eagles* into an air-to-air combat range over the Atlantic to engage ten Navy fighter jets in a dog fight. While imbibing spirits and exuding bravado at the Air Force Officers Club, four versus ten is what we Air Force guys commonly referred to as a fair fight.

Our four-ship of *Eagles* spread into tactical formation and began parceling up the targets that were coming right at us into the morning sun. My flight leader assigned me the right flank, and I selected two targets flying in trail, a common Soviet tactic. I flew a stern conversion and killed the trailer with a simulated AIM-9 *Sidewinder* heat shot.

"Fox Two!"

Simulated splash. There wasn't time to celebrate the kill, because the leader was maneuvering hard. I tangled with him for a few turns before I killed him with the gun.

"Fox Three!"

I wanted to go after a third bandit, but I had been predictable too long. The Squids (our nickname for Navy fighter pilots) were good, and they'd love nothing more than to bag an *Eagle* that had tracked its prey too long.

I lit the burners and pulled straight up into the blue sky, straining to check my six o'clock to make sure no bandits were on my tail. My six was clear, but the stick felt odd. I had expected stick pressure to lighten up as my airspeed melted away in the vertical climb. Instead, the stick was rock solid. I glanced inside the cockpit to check my speed. The altimeter was a blur. I was doing Mach 2.2 straight down! That's almost 1,700 miles an hour. At that speed, I could fly from Philadelphia to Washington, D.C. in about five minutes instead of two-and-a-half hours by car. If I flew at Mach 2.2 all the way down from 35,000 feet, I'd be a grease spot on the ocean in fewer than 14 seconds.

Understand that I calculated the speeds above in the comfort of the O Club bar *after* the flight, not while I was actually plummeting to earth at an alarmingly rapid rate. I double checked my numbers: yep, 14 seconds until I would've become a grease spot.

Being a cunning aviator with a bright future, I didn't want to become a grease spot. I pulled the throttles to idle and deployed the speed brake. My helmet slammed forward, and I heard a loud bang. Excess air pressure had broken the speed brake and slammed it shut. Of course, I was pulling on the pole big time. At first, I could get only 3.5 *G*s, but, as the speed decayed, available *G* increased. I pulled out of the dive as soon as aerodynamic forces let me. I selected burners and climbed back into the fight. I figured that I had skipped being shark bait by two seconds.

During the flight back to Langley, my hands began to tremble. Then my knees. I noticed that I had lowered my seat during the unintentional supersonic dive. Doubting the outcome at some point, my instincts must have told me to block the view of the water so I wouldn't die tensed up. (Any fighter pilot prefers a serene appearance in his coffin in order to leave a favorable last impression.)

I wasn't some new guy on the block on the day the whole world turned blue. I had often mixed it up in air-to-air dog fights, yet, I had become disoriented long enough for the Reaper to take a swing at me. Thank God for a magnificent airplane and a second chance.

Frank T. Courtney
London, England
Captain, Royal Flying Corps
Curtiss-Wright Corporation
Convair
The Boeing Company

CHAPTER 18

PATIENCE

THE REAPER'S IMPATIENCE sometimes foils his designs on the life of an aviator, as it did when Frank T. Courtney's Rolls-Royce engine abruptly quit scarcely a moment before he committed to open ocean.

In the early days of aviation, the 20-mile segment from Dover, England to Le Gris Nez, France (Straits of Dover) was one of the most heavily-traveled air route segments in the world. Pilots wanted to minimize the time they spent over water because rapid-response sea rescue was non-existent. Ditching in the English Channel was synonymous with death by hypothermia and drowning. Even as late as 1940, nearly 200 Royal Air Force fighter pilots died from exposure to the Channel's frigid temperatures during the Battle of Britain.

Throughout history, the Channel had been a momentous obstacle to the armies of Caesar, Napoleon, and Hitler. It was a serious threat to the longevity of pioneering pilots, too. Courtney referred to the Channel as Britain's "turbulent ditch."

In 1922 there were no electronic aids for navigation. Pilots relied on visual cues. The term *IMC* – instrument meteorological conditions – didn't exist because there weren't any relevant instruments. Frequently occurring heavy clouds, rain, and fog forced pilots to cross the Channel by skimming across the tops of barely discernable waves.

Occasionally pilots successfully crossed the Channel only to discover that they had no way to climb above the height of cliffs that towered over either end of the Straits. In such cases, the pilots stayed low in visual meteorological conditions (VMC) and turned left or right in search of a coastal airport sufficiently free of clouds to land. Mishaps were common as pilots pressed the limits of contact flying at low altitudes in marginal weather. One French pilot landed at Croydon, England trailing several feet of telegraph wire from his landing gear.

In gale winds and blinding rain one foul day in 1921, Courtney was about to cross the Channel with three passengers on a Brussels-to-London flight in a Westland *Limousine*. Shortly before dropping over the cliffs at Cape Gris Nez to skim across the tops of a raging sea, his engine quit. After making an emergency landing in a muddy field near the cliffs, he discovered that a partially open drain cock had emptied his fuel tank well ahead of schedule. If the engine had run out of fuel two minutes later, Courtney would have been forced to ditch in the Channel, resulting in four deaths.

Virtues may lie hidden among the Reaper's loathsome nature, but, on this day at least, *patience* wasn't one of them.

Historical Addendum

Although he was shot down during World War I by German ace Max Immelmann, Courtney survived to become the leader of England's "Suicide Club Squadron." He subsequently became a test pilot in England and the United States. He died in 1982 at the age of 88.

Courtney, Frank T. *The Eighth Sea.* Doubleday, 1972.

Photo courtesy of John Ransom

John Ransom

Clearwater, Florida
Purdue University
Itinerant Airline Pilot
Lockheed L-188 *Electra*, B-727, DC-7,
DC-9, DC-10, B-737, B-757, B-767, MD-11
Purdue Airlines, Quickway Air Service,
Century 2000 Air Travel Club, Air Florida,
Arrow Air, Midway Airlines, United Airlines,
United Parcel Service

CHAPTER 19

GEORGE

"UP THE GEAR!" the taciturn Captain said.

The Douglas DC-7 was still lumbering down the runway like an elephant on a pogo stick with the nose gear barely off the ground. I had heard the command "gear up" hundreds of times and it had always, *always* been in the air. I had never heard the almost Shakespearian command "up the gear" until now, and, being on the ground, I didn't like it much.

In 1971, oceanic shipping was immobilized by a strike sanctioned by the International Longshore and Warehouse Union (ILWU). Caribbean islanders (citizens of Puerto Rico in particular) were in dire need of food. The ensuing airlift gave me an opportunity to add some much-needed "heavy" flight time to my log book. I was asked to fly relief flights to San Juan as the First Officer of a DC-7C painted in Saturn Airways colors – a big red stripe down the side with a red circle on the tail. The only other marking was the registration number, N90804. I was an adventurous, altruistic guy, so I accepted.

I was full of low-timer's optimism as I strolled across the ramp toward the 140,000-pound, four-engine DC-7. Parked beside it was a flatbed tractor-trailer loaded with eight thousand chickens in tiny cages. The journey from Pennsylvania to Miami was the first major road trip for these Quaker State egg-layers, and they were showing signs of acute stress. Workers had to load the cages individually through the main entry door, because, even though the passenger-configured plane had been stripped of its seats, it didn't have a cargo door. By the time loading was complete, the cabin temperature had reached 120 degrees Fahrenheit.

The distressed hens didn't fare any better in the air, either. The DC-7 air-conditioning system couldn't cope with the heat at lower altitudes, and the cabin got even hotter. Over Bimini, our quick-thinking flight engineer removed over-wing exits to improve air flow. The cabin temperature went down, but at the expense of creating a blinding feather-storm for the remainder of the flight. Workers who off-loaded our flock of sparsely-feathered friends discovered that only three thousand hens had survived.

I continued flying DC-7 relief flights, but without the appalling loss of life. My full-time job at the time was flight instruction, teaching students to fly Cessna 150s, sometimes successfully. My "heavy" experience prior to flying the DC-7 consisted mostly of DC-6 simulator time and flying as a student first officer on DC-9s. The owner of N90804 didn't seem to mind my lack of DC-7 training or flying experience. He leased the airplane to a local operator on the condition that I would stay with the aircraft to represent his interests. I learned a lot flying N90804. For example, on my maiden flight delivering furniture to St. Kitts, Virgin Islands, I learned that heavy piston-engine airliners are much, much more complicated to operate than jets. I vowed to stay away from heavy piston-engine airliners if at all possible.

By the time I met George, I had a dozen DC-7 Miami-San Juan round trips under my belt. The flights originated from the northwest portion of Miami International Airport called "Corrosion Corner." I was told that my flights were at night because the cooler temperatures provided better aircraft performance. The truth was that night flights avoided interactions with pesky Federal Aviation Administration (FAA) personnel, most of whom worked daylight hours only. (As a rule, I learned, any ramp with an FAA car in sight was an empty ramp.)

I carried my spiffy, brand-new Jeppesen brown-leather flight bag to the DC-7 cockpit, past Bill, the flight engineer, and placed it to the right of the co-pilot's seat. To my left, Captain George was passively observing freight being loaded onto a DC-6 and L-1049 *Connies* out on the bustling ramp.

"We're all filed," I said.

George just glanced at me, nodded, and looked back out the window. He was not a chatty fellow. Aviation's Calvin Coolidge. I put him in his mid-sixties. He seemed pensive to the point of disinterest. He had no professional curiosity concerning tasks delegated to other crew members. Frivolous details like our cargo of 40,000 pounds of frozen pork and the general condition of the aircraft couldn't compete with the comfort of his seat. He was indifferent to the routing to San Juan, destination weather, and other flight plan information, too. He couldn't have been more aloof during engine start.

I wasn't sure which checklist to use. I had been using an old Saturn Airways checklist that lived on the airplane. I also had located a BOAC flight manual and checklist tucked away in a box containing the periscopic sextant. Bill, a National Airlines Boeing 727 flight engineer, and I would have been glad to use any checklist George directed. Still, George hadn't shown a preference for checklists or anything else. He pushed the throttles up to taxi away from Corrosion Corner.

"Standard Airlift," is all he said.

We assumed that George wanted us to use Airlift International checklists, but, in time, we came to reckon that

George's meaning was broader. In retrospect, I believe that George wanted us to do things the way he remembered having done them during his days at Airlift International. In other words, "Standard Airlift" was George's version of a crew briefing that, at the time, was incomprehensible to Bill and me.

Bill and I went through the Saturn checklist for the run-ups, and then George lined us up on Runway Nine Left for departure. I still wasn't sure who was going to handle the controls on this flight, so I asked, as casually as possible, "You flying?"

George, who was gazing down the runway like a visionary contemplating the future, just nodded.

"Douglas Eight-Oh-Four, Runway Nine Left, cleared for takeoff."

As George pushed up his set of throttles, Bill adjusted my set to squeeze out all the power possible from the Curtiss-Wright Cyclone 3350 turbo-compound engines. The airplane creaked down the runway, accelerating to eighty knots, at which point George transitioned his left hand from the nose-gear steering wheel to the yoke. We continued to accelerate. George pulled back the yoke to rotate, and we felt the nose gear strut partially extend. At that instant, George released his throttles, stretched his right hand out over the pedestal, palm up, and said, "Up the gear."

First of all, I'd never heard anyone say, "Up the Gear." I'd always heard, "Gear Up." My first thought was, yes, it's different, but it's kind of cool, too. I briefly considered adopting this unusual affectation to be considered cool when I eventually became a captain. My second thought, however, and it was a much more immediately relevant thought, was that George was telling us to retract the gear while the airplane was still on the ground, substantially on the ground.

It didn't take a genius to figure out that it was too early to retract the gear. In most aircraft, the gear handle is located on the instrument panel in front of the first officer. If that had been the case, I would have simply delayed moving the gear handle up until I knew we were airborne, regardless of what the captain said. But this wasn't the case. This was a DC-7, and on a DC-7 the gear handle is on the aft side of the pedestal and is operated by the flight engineer. Bill, the engineer, didn't have nearly the vantage point that I did to see that we were still firmly on the runway. Luckily, Bill had been around, and the nerve endings in his buttocks told him we were still on the runway. His right hand squeezed my upper left arm as if to ask, "Really?"

I shook my head rapidly enough to give myself a headache to make sure he got the message.

Message received. He squeezed the gear handle release a few times as if attempting to retract the gear, but he never moved it up.

George repeated his command, as well as his sweeping arm motion: "Up the gear!" This time he said it with more gusto.

Bill and I could feel the main gear struts extend. We were – presumably – airborne. Bill waited for me to confirm the action. Without looking back at him, I shrugged half-heartedly, so he finally moved the handle up, and the gear began to retract.

Normally, after gear retraction and after gaining a little altitude, the flying pilot would call for METO power. (METO stands for Maximum Except Take Off, a power setting that's less than maximum power but more than climb power). METO power is still hard on the engines and is designed to be used for a minute or two until selecting climb power for the remainder of the climb to cruising altitude.

Climb power was considerably less than METO power and much less demanding of the engines.

This is why Bill and I were both surprised (and confused) when George made his next callout: "Climb Power." The landing gear were still in transit. Of even greater concern, we were still below roof level of the George T. Baker Aviation School building straight ahead of us on Le Jeune Road. Because the building was straight ahead of us, it was getting larger by the second. With takeoff flaps extended, gear in transit, cowl flaps wide-open, and our slow speed, climb power was woefully inadequate. George reached down to nudge his throttles back.

Hoping to communicate wordlessly once again with Bill, I rapidly shook my head. (It was actually more of a blur than a shake.) Bill was well ahead of me. He reached up as George began retarding the throttles and limited their travel so we lost no more than a couple of inches of manifold pressure.

"METO?" Bill asked.

"Climb power. Gotta save these engines," George said.

Apparently, smashing into the Baker Aviation School *today* was a lower priority risk in George's opinion than the chance of overcooking the four engines *tomorrow*. Bill parroted the climb power command, but he reduced the power only slowly, only reluctantly, and only to about METO anyway.

True to his nonconforming style, George called for flap retraction at too low an altitude. Once again, Bill responded at a snail's pace in the interest of our longevity. A minute or so later, while overflying Interstate 95, Bill finally, and almost imperceptibly, brought the throttles back to climb power. By the time we passed over Bimini at just over 1,000 feet, the possibility that George was suicidal had occurred to me more than once. Or was there a deeper meaning to his eccentric behavior that I was missing?

Photo credit: icholakov01/depositphotos.com

Douglas DC-7

The rest of the climb was comparatively uneventful. As we leveled off at cruise altitude over the Bahamas, George nodded in my direction and took his hands off the yoke. He just stopped flying without a word. Dawn was breaking so I barely saw his head nod. If it had still been dark, I wouldn't have known about the change of flying duties, and N90804 would have kept on boring holes in the sky all by itself with no one at the controls.

Normally, if the captain needed to sleep *en route*, he would climb into one of the bunks and the flight engineer would occupy the vacant captain's seat. But there was nothing normal about this flight. George slept soundly right there in his seat. This meant that I was as busy as a one-armed juggler making position reports on HF radio and tuning NDBs so we could navigate down Amber 17. A little past Grand Turk, George began to stir. He put his hands on the yoke, which I took to mean that I was no longer flying the airplane.

"Starting down," George said.

We were still a couple of hundred miles from San Juan, so we were starting our descent about 150 miles early. Bill was rummaging around in the back of the cockpit, so I called him up so he could do some mysterious flight engineer tasks associated with descents. He mentioned to George that we could remain at cruise altitude for quite a while longer.

"Cylinder Heads," George said.

We started down.

Although George seemed not to care, I had qualms about descending without an Air Traffic Control clearance, so I busily tried to get a clearance from San Juan. We were too low and far out for clear communications. San Juan was garbled and getting worse because of our descent, so I winged it. I fabricated a clearance read-back.

"Roger," I said, "descend and maintain three thousand."

Cylinder heads of piston-powered airliners could be coddled by descending at low rates of descent. If that's what George meant by his "cylinder head" comment, he didn't follow through, because he set up a descent of 600 feet per minute. At this rate, cylinder head temperatures would drop rapidly, as ours were doing, judging from the popping sounds they were making. Bill persuaded George to reduce the descent rate to 400 feet per minute to protect the engines. Although we leveled off at three thousand feet way ahead of profile, what a spectacular view of the ocean we had! It took us another thirty minutes to see any hint of land. Fortunately, I was able to get an Eastern DC-8 to confirm with San Juan that we were, indeed, cleared to three thousand feet.

George started slowing the aircraft down using a process called "flying with your mouth." The idea was for the flying pilot to call for a power setting and the flight engineer would set it using the throttles. Brake Mean Effective Pressure (BMEP) was the conventional reference measure of power used.

"Gimme one-twenty-five," George said.

Bill set BMEP at 125. So, there we were, 15 miles from the airport bumbling around barely above stall speed.

"One-twenty."

Bill set 120. I thought I could feel airframe buffet.

"One-fifteen."

Bill wanted no part of "one-fifteen." He pushed BMEP up to 125.

I never had experienced the onset of a stall in a DC-7, but I'd ridden through countless stalls in Cessna 150s. I knew what pre-stall buffet felt like. I was feeling it now.

"Better make it one-twenty," George said.

Bill fudged a little and pushed it up to 135. The buffeting stopped. George had given up some altitude to make the buffeting go away, so, as we more-or-less lined up for final approach, the runway looked a lot flatter than I was accustomed to seeing it. I told George that we were full-scale deflection low on the glideslope.

Unconcerned, George continued to descend. He called for flaps and then for 120. Even though Bill gave him 130, we remained dangerously low and slow.

"Down the gear!"

I should've known *that* was coming but somehow it sneaked up on me. We were now well below a thousand feet above the ground, and, while the gear was in transit, George called out his last configuration change.

"Flaps!"

We were still well below the glide slope, fully configured, and approximately lined up with the runway. There was a chance we might survive whatever happened next. George slowly grasped that we were both low *and* slow, so he made a final power call.

"One-thirty!"

Bill pushed BMEP well beyond 145. He may have reached METO for all I knew.

Here, a quick overview of a normal DC-7 landing is in order. In landing configuration, the DC-7 attitude is slightly nose-down, so the plan, as the airplane nears the runway, is to gently bring the nose up to level while slowly reducing power. A *gradual* power reduction ensures enough speed until touchdown and allows the large propellers to provide added airflow over the wings. It's normally a smooth, unhurried maneuver. There was nothing smooth, unhurried, or normal about this approach.

As we passed over the fence, our nose was alarmingly high. Our engines were screaming and our sink rate was increasing. I strained to think of a way to avoid incipient disaster, but, like General Custer's scouts at the Little Bighorn, I came up empty-handed. Going around wasn't going to work since we were already carrying max power and were still descending. I focused on keeping my wits about me so I would be ready to make a clean getaway during evacuation from the inevitable wreckage.

Just as I figured things couldn't get worse, George abruptly pushed forward on the yoke, pulled the throttles back all the way to the stops, and then yanked the yoke smartly back into his gut. It's exactly what a *kamikaze* would have done.

Bill and I grabbed hold of whatever we could. I sensed Bill's death grip on my seatback cushion. The glare shield flexed under the vice-like clutch of my fingers. I had never clenched anything tighter in my life. We braced for what would come next.

What came next was one of the sweetest DC-7 landings I had ever experienced. It was *supernaturally* smooth, if you ignore the thump from the slight tail strike. I interpreted George's grunt as satisfaction as he reached down to open the reverse gate. Abandoning any previous pretense about saving the engines, he yanked the throttles into reverse. Number four engine immediately auto-feathered and started gushing oil all over the runway. One of the other engines backfired like a howitzer shot. The airplane shook and shuddered because of the excessive reverse and heavy braking. Miraculously, we still had three operative engines as we lumbered off the runway onto a high-speed taxiway. For the first time all day, George was animated and loquacious.

"I'll teach you boys how to fly this airplane!" he shouted with a delirious falsetto cackle at the end like ... maybe ... Rasputin.

Is it possible to be so happy that you cry? As I sensed the Grim Reaper passing me by, I had to think so.

Photo credit: Kevin Griffin & lp2studio/123RF.com

Iceal E. "Gene" Hambleton

Tucson, Arizona
1918-2004
Lieutenant Colonel, United States Air Force
B-29, EB-66

CHAPTER 20

RESCUE

LIKE MANY SURVIVORS of air disasters, Air Force Lt. Col. Gene Hambleton often pondered why he was the only member of his six-man aircrew to dodge the wrath of the Grim Reaper on March 30, 1972. He alone ejected safely from an EB-66 *Destroyer* blown out of the sky by a North Vietnamese SA-2 surface-to-air missile. Hambleton, a veteran of World War II, the Korean War, and the Vietnam War, knew all too well that the Reaper wasn't finished with him yet.

Hambleton's job was a combination of electronic warfare officer, copilot, engineer, and navigator. He was no newcomer to hostile fire, having flown 63 combat missions in Southeast Asia. At 53 years of age, he was older than the fathers of the four electronic warfare officers (nicknamed "Crows") who were positioned behind him in the EB-66. The Crows were electronically sweeping the area south of the Demilitarized Zone (DMZ) for enemy signals in preparation for an inbound cell of American B-52 bombers. When the Crows detected enemy electronic signals, they jammed them to diminish the missile threat to American fighters and bombers.

With little warning, the warhead of a North Vietnamese SA-2 *Guideline* exploded near Hambleton's EB-66. He managed to eject from the aircraft as it broke apart. The first challenge he faced, after being blasted into sub-freezing temperatures at 30,000 feet, was a spinning ejection seat. Centrifugal forces and hypoxia were shrinking his time of useful consciousness, so, before passing out, he manually deployed his parachute and activated his emergency oxygen bottle. A billowing chute and seat separation stabilized his trajectory and the oxygen helped clear his mind. He could breathe again, but his core body temperature was dropping fast, causing him to shiver uncontrollably.

Hambleton finally reached a zone of humid tropical air at lower altitudes. When he regained the use of his nearly frozen fingers, he dressed his wounds and stemmed bleeding from his right index finger. Still descending in his chute, he used his survival radio to contact an Air Force Forward Air Controller (FAC) whom he could see flying in an orbit around him. This chance encounter raised Hambleton's hopes for being rescued quickly, perhaps a few minutes after landing in the jungle below. As the next couple of minutes played out, however, prospects for a speedy extraction faded fast.

Unfortunately, the Demilitarized Zone (DMZ) wasn't demilitarized. North Vietnam had staged a massive invasion of the Republic of Vietnam, and Hambleton was descending right into the center of their positions. He hit the ground on the edge of a dry rice paddy and immediately took cover. He radioed the FAC, who coordinated rescue efforts. Withering hostile fire faced each American aircraft that responded, so the rescue effort had to stand down as night approached. Hambleton used his knife to dig in. He was hungry, thirsty, and scared to death by the almost constant sound of big guns all around him.

Hambleton was a missile expert with a top secret clearance, so capturing him was a high-priority for the North

Vietnamese and the Russians. Hambleton wasn't about to give them the satisfaction of taking him alive, but he wasn't keen to end his own life as a preventative measure, either. A resourceful American aviator was pitted against 40,000 North Vietnamese soldiers in a fight that would take 12 days to resolve.

The following morning dawned and the North Vietnamese continued to fight off every rescue attempt made by the Americans. Close air support fighters and helicopters took heavy fire, and one helicopter was shot down. For a dozen days Hambleton endured rain, heat, hunger, thirst, sickness, pain, swarms of mosquitoes, encounters with snakes, repeated close calls with enemy infantry, big guns, artillery, and tanks to stay on the move a step ahead of his determined pursuers. When enemy patrols closed in on his hiding places beneath rotting jungle foliage, he willed himself to be as motionless as a statue. No mosquito or even an enemy soldier pissing on him could make him move.

Hambleton's survival was a seminar on improvisation. On a night when he thought he couldn't last another 24 hours without food, he discovered a cornfield. He stuffed ears of sweet corn into his flight suit pockets. He took refuge behind lines of "gravel" dropped by A-1 *Sandies*. Gravel was a form of land mine that provided a barrier between Hambleton and North Vietnamese patrols. The enemy shipped in mine-sweepers and they exerted constant pressure on Hambleton by finding and destroying his protective strip of land mines. On the ninth day of his evasion, when attacked by a Vietnamese in the dead of night, Hambleton retaliated by killing him with his knife.

The Air Force tried every idea they could think of to neutralize the area around Hambleton enough to send a helicopter in for extraction. Psychological warfare C-130 *Hercules* aircraft blasted the enemy with powerful loudspeakers all night long. AC-130 *Specters*, brimming with machine guns and 20-mm Gatling guns, saved Hambleton from capture several times. He survived strings of bombs laid down by B-52s to protect him from searchers and to give the impression that the United States had given up attempts to rescue him. The ploy worked for a short time even if the bombs were so close that they blew Hambleton's helmet off and temporarily deafened him. Because of targeting information radioed from Hambleton to the FAC, B-52s were able to destroy several big guns and an SA-2 *Guideline* launching site.

Hambleton's perspectives changed. In the past, he had shared drinks with F-4 *Phantom* pilots at various Officer Club bars, and he had referred to them as "blowtorch jockies" and guys "in cowboy boots ... who all seemed to hail from Texas." But, during his ordeal, as he watched the *Phantoms* drop their ordnance precisely on the targets he had radioed to the FAC, he stopped caring about their footwear or where they came from; he just wanted to live long enough to buy them a drink at the O Club bar.

The twelve-day rescue operation was the largest and most difficult such effort undertaken during the Vietnam War. During attempts to extract Hambleton, five American airplanes were shot down, nine airframes were badly damaged, 11 American rescuers were killed in action, and two rescuers were captured by the North Vietnamese. Despite this heavy toll, rescue efforts continued, but in a different form. A gutsy South Vietnamese commando and a fearless Navy SEAL, Lt. JG Tom Morris, infiltrated enemy lines on a narrow boat called a sampan at great personal risk on a mission to free Hambleton. They were well-trained and cautious. They took cover from enemy search parties in coves and river banks overgrown with brush.

Hambleton feared that his eleventh day of evading three divisions of enemy infantry would be his last. He was too hungry and too sleep-deprived to be sure he was thinking clearly. As a last ditch effort to get past dozens of hostile troops, Hambleton was clutching a slippery railroad tie floating downriver when he spotted a threat that used up every drop of adrenalin that remained in his body. He came face-to-face with a water snake. The Loch Ness monster couldn't have been more frightening. Against every impulse, Hambleton remained motionless to avoid giving away his position. The snake ignored him and swam away without making his worst dreams come true. Hambleton's nerves were shot. He barely had enough energy to reach the muddy river bank and wallow in the muck to camouflage himself before collapsing.

A short time later, a Vietnamese sampan paddled into view from around a bend in the river. Hambleton had sustained his will to fight through days of trials and disappointments, but, as the boat drew nearer, he accepted the reality that he was out of options. He gathered himself, cradling his knife for one last lunge as he watched the sampan's approach. Filthy, fatigued, and famished, Hambleton trembled in anticipation of his final violent act.

The sampan glided to a spot just beyond his reach. A lone Vietnamese paddler eyed Hambleton impassively. A motion beneath a stack of banana leaves in the middle of the boat attracted Hambleton's attention. He examined the stack of leaves warily. Peering at him from beneath the shadows of the pile of leaves was a pair of eyes, non-Asian eyes.

"What's your dog's name?" a voice asked in English.

"Pierre," Hambleton said, perhaps as astonished to see round eyes beneath a pile of banana leaves as he was at his recall of the answer to one of his identification security questions. The camouflaged SEAL gave Hambleton water and helped him hide beneath banana leaves. The Vietnamese paddler reversed directions and silently hugged the thick foliage of the river bank to travel downstream without attracting attention.

Each time the three evaders encountered ambushes, the SEAL called in airstrikes. *Phantom* Gatling guns growled and high explosive incendiary bullets tore the North Vietnamese search teams to pieces. When the SEAL's radio went dead, Hambleton offered up his survival radio. The SEAL used the last of the radio's battery charge to call in another air strike. The sampan crept on down-river. Hambleton could hear bullets from snipers hit the water around the little boat. He could even hear machetes slashing through jungle growth as enemy search parties relentlessly sought to find him. Through it all, Hambleton stayed motionless underneath his hot, humid, insect-infested shelter of banana leaves.

At last, the sampan slid onto a shallow bank littered with piles of river debris and scattered bushes. Hambleton peeked over the gunwales of the boat in time to see the bushes move. Camouflaged South Vietnamese Marines appeared to escort the three evaders to a remote concrete bunker, unused for almost two decades since the withdrawal of French forces. The South Vietnamese rescuers treated Hambleton's wounds, gave him water, and massaged his feet until he could walk again. Meanwhile, the SEAL continued to coordinate airstrikes to suppress enemy troops all around them. A personnel carrier arrived and a Vietnamese Marine and the SEAL carried Hambleton aboard on a stretcher. The armored personnel carrier jostled and lurched through the jungle while Hambleton was perforated like a voodoo doll by needles for intravenous fluids and morphine. In a clearing in the jungle, a *Jolly Green Giant* was waiting to airlift

Hambleton to the 388th Tactical Fighter Wing hospital at Da Nang.

Even in the hospital, Hambleton's adventures weren't over. Admiral Thomas Moorer, Chairman of the Joint Chiefs of Staff, called to extend congratulations. Moorer vividly remembered being shot down by the Japanese in 1942, and he had a special insight into the challenges of surviving such an ordeal. Not long after the Admiral's call, Hambleton was blown out of his hospital bed onto his fractured arm by an exploding rocket that was part of a North Vietnamese attack. After Hambleton was airlifted to the Philippines, the Grim Reaper took another swipe at him. One of the worst earthquakes in decades almost destroyed the American medical facility where he was being treated.

Many years after his extraordinary escape and after his medical retirement from the Air Force, Hambleton often reflected on his extraction with mixed feelings about the human cost to save him. He collaborated with former Air Force Colonel William C. Anderson to publish a book titled *Bat 21* about his dramatic evasion behind enemy lines. Anderson, author of over 20 books and two screenplays, published details of an elaborate method Air Force Intelligence and Hambleton used to exchange ground navigation information. The FAC radioed the number of a specific golf hole that Hambleton had played as a coded method of giving compass directions and distances to the downed aviator. When Hambleton reached the objective of a hole, he could report reaching "the green" without giving away his location to enemy radio monitors. The technique was fully revealed in a film starring Gene Hackman and Danny Glover.

On several public occasions, Hambleton respectfully expressed his great sorrow for the men who died to extract him from the grip of the Reaper. Until his death in 2004, he bore a debt of profound gratitude for their courage and sacrifice.

Anderson, William C. *Bat 21*. Bantam Books, 1983.

Photo credit: apostrophe & nyvltart/123RF.com

George H. W. "Skin" Bush

Milton, Massachusetts
Yale University
Lieutenant JG, United States Navy
TBM *Avenger*
United States House of Representatives (Texas)
Ambassador to the United Nations
Head of the American Liaison Office in China
CIA Director
Vice-President of the United States
President of the United States

CHAPTER 21

TIMING

ELUDING THE GRASP of the Grim Reaper can depend on a split-second decision executed at exactly the right moment in the midst of pandemonium, as in this story from 1944 involving the American Navy's youngest World War II aviator, Lieutenant JG George H. W. Bush.

Some 600 miles southeast of Tokyo, the craggy island of Chichi Jima was vital to Japanese operations at Iwo Jima, the Palaus, and Leyte. Using Korean and Chinese slave laborers, the Japanese military had constructed seven 200-foot antennas on Chichi Jima's Mount Yoake. The island was fortified by 15,000 soldiers, three extensive underground bunkers, a radar site, dozens of anti-aircraft guns, and 166 suicide boats.

The United States Navy's aerial attacks against Chichi Jima on September 1, 1944 were unsuccessful. The next day, the Navy sent another attacking force of F6F *Hellcats* and TBM *Avengers*. (The *Avenger* was a torpedo bomber that also could drop depth charges and conventional bombs.) Despite intense anti-aircraft gunfire, LT JG George Bush rolled his TBM into a thirty-five-degree dive bomb attack. Although he put his bombs on target, a burst of flak set his engine on fire.

The timing of Bush's decision to bail out of the burning *Avenger* was critical. Bailing out too soon would have almost certainly resulted in the capture of Bush and his two crewmembers. Delaying the bailout decision allowed Bush to fly further away from Japanese forces on the island toward United States Navy submarines assigned to rescue duty. Every second's delay, however, increased chances that the *Avenger* would blow up. Every second's delay decreased chances of proper parachute deployment.

Bush was well-equipped to make such decisions. He had flown more than 50 combat sorties and made more than a hundred cable-arrested landings on the carrier *USS San Jacinto*. Bush had flown sorties against Wake Island, Saipan, Peleliu, and Tinian. Just six weeks earlier, during a 400-plane Japanese strike against the *San Jacinto's* battle group, Bush's *Avenger* had been hit as he dropped a depth charge on top of a Japanese submarine. Bush was forced to ditch the aircraft. Bush served the remaining days of the "Great Marianas Turkey Shoot" aboard the ship that rescued him from the ocean, the *USS C. K. Bronson*.

Bush nursed the burning plane away from Chichi Jima and gave the command to bail out at the last possible moment. His parachute barely deployed before his impact with the ocean. Neither RM2 John Delaney nor LT JG William White survived the experience. The *Avenger* blew up shortly after their egress. Bush smashed his head against the horizontal stabilizer during bailout and his parachute was damaged by the aircraft empennage so his landing on the surface of the ocean was a hard one. He was dazed but aware that he was losing a lot of blood because of his head injury and jelly fish stings to his hands.

He swam quickly to his one-man raft, boarded it, and paddled in the opposite direction from pursuing Japanese vessels. He might have paddled harder if he had known about reports of Japanese soldiers murdering downed airmen to eat their flesh. A Navy fighter dropped a medical kit to him so he could sterilize his multiple wounds. Severe pain from his head injuries caused him to vomit for three solid hours until the submarine *USS Finback* emerged from the 3,500-foot deep Bonin Trench and rescued him.

Bush built a career on making tough decisions. After the war he was named captain of the Yale University baseball team that finished second to the University of Southern California in the college World Series. He went on to be elected to the highest office in the land. None of his achievements would have been fulfilled had he not thwarted the Reaper's grisly plan with bold decisiveness at a critical moment in a dire situation.

Parmet, Herbert S. *George Bush: The Life of a Lone Star Yankee.* Scribner, 1977.

James D. "Bogie" Bogenrief

Watertown, South Dakota
Red Wing, Minnesota
Minnesota State University, Mankato
Colonel, United States Air Force
F-4C, D, E, K, M

CHAPTER 22

LINE OF SUCCESSION

THE GRIM REAPER doesn't always go for a quick kill. Like a cat toying with a mouse, the Reaper sometimes messes around with you to see whether you'll do the job yourself. That's what happened to me one sunny afternoon in Spain shortly after takeoff from Torrejón Air Base in my trusty F-4C *Phantom II*.

BANG!

From my Weapon Systems Officer's position in the back seat, the loud report sounded like a compressor stall. Hell, it sounded more like a bomb going off next to my forehead. A 400-knot blast of wind buffeting my helmet was a clue that this was something bigger than a compressor stall. In an instant, the front canopy was gone. My jet began to roll left, away from the formation leader. Not only was the front canopy AWOL, it appeared that the pilot, Captain Tom Steerman, had followed suit! I shook the stick side-to-side, a gesture that roughly translated to, "You up there?"

I got no response from Tom, so I turned the radio volume to maximum and shouted to him on the intercom. Still no reply. It dawned on me that my "nose gunner" was either incapacitated or absent and that I, next in the line of succession, was in a pickle.

Executive summary: I was a thousand feet above the city of Alcalá de Henares loaded with12 practice bombs, a

147

Gatling gun, and two wing tanks full of fuel in a *Phantom* missing a front canopy and a pilot. I was fortunate to have a stick in the back seat. Navy and Marine Corps F-4 Radar Intercept Officers didn't have sticks in the back, so, in the same circumstances, they would have had no alternative but to punch out. I had logged a lot of back seat flying time; now it was time to put my proficiency to work. I radioed the formation leader.

"Lead, this is Two Bravo. I'll climb to two-thousand-five-hundred. Can you do a visual check on Two Alpha?"

Lead barrel rolled over the top of my plane so he could see down into the front cockpit.

"Two Bravo, you're alone in the jet. The front seat's in place, but we can't see Two Alpha anywhere. State your intentions."

From the rear seat, I wasn't able to jettison external wing fuel tanks. I couldn't lower gear, flaps, or the tail hook normally, either. I told Lead that I'd burn off fuel to reduce my gross weight below the maximum for landing, use emergency air bottles to blow down landing gear and flaps, and pull a circuit breaker to drop the tail hook. I half expected my ejection seat to spontaneously blow me out of the cockpit at any moment. Flying formation at a reduced speed of 250 knots for forty-five minutes to burn off gas might sound monotonous, but I wasn't bored at all. First of all, communicating was difficult because the wind blast was thunderously loud even at reduced air speed. Second of all, every commander with farts-and-darts on his hat within a hundred miles got in on the act. I might have been missing a canopy, but I wasn't short of advice. I received more guidance in half an hour than some people get in a lifetime. The supervisor of flying (SOF), three squadron commanders, the chief of standardization and evaluation, the director of operations, the wing commander, and some guy at Sixteenth Air Force all chimed in. It wouldn't have surprised me if the Secretary of Defense had jumped in with his two cents.

I told Lead that Tower should clear the traffic pattern before my approach because taking the cable would close the runway for a while. Lead concurred. He led me on a couple of straight-in approaches so I could get a sight picture of what the landing attitude would look like. I asked Lead to carry an extra ten knots on final for the sake of my kids (as yet unborn). He agreed and, when all traffic was cleared out of our way, he lined me up for a ten-mile straight-in approach. I radioed him that I was ready to blow down the gear. Like magic, before I could blow the gear down, the landing gear lowered normally without any action on my part. Tom was still up front! He had regained consciousness, heard my radio transmission, and responded to my radio call by lowering the gear using the normal gear handle. I shook the stick. This time, Tom replied by shaking the stick also. I told Lead that Tom had lowered the gear. Lead closed in for another look into the front cockpit.

"Two Bravo, I can see Two Alpha now. He's hunched over beneath the instrument panel."

I imagined a pretzel in a green Nomex flight suit contorted to avoid being sucked out of the cockpit like a piece of lint by a vacuum cleaner. Authorities on the ground started asking questions. Could I communicate with Tom? Did I need an ambulance? What was my fuel state?

I told Tom by intercom to shake the stick if he could hear me through the ferocious noise of the wind blast. Like me, he could hear with difficulty, but he still couldn't transmit. I told him to shake the stick if he could deploy the drogue chute on landing. He did. Because Tom would be able to pop the drogue chute, I told Lead that I could land on his wing (fly formation until touchdown).

We touched down in formation on Runway Zero Five. Tom deployed our chute right away and, after gaining five seconds of separation, Lead popped his. I cleared the runway at the end and stopped in the de-arm area. All the heavy hitters had left the command post and were there to greet us (or view the weenie roast if I had screwed up). A terrorist bomb could have wiped out the 401st Tactical Fighter Wing's entire leadership structure and two wind-blown aviators. Rotating beacons flashed on top of fire trucks and an ambulance. The only people missing from the welcoming committee were chaplains, cheerleaders, and a band.

The ambulance, whose crew included a nurse who was an incredibly hot young lady, took Tom off to the hospital. There were no young ladies of any description where I was going. Back in the squadron offices I was interrogated well beyond the time at which I had planned to be guzzling adult beverages at the Officers Club bar. My powerful thirst had to wait so all the second guessers could pile on. The greatest beneficiary of my adventure was the owner of a walled villa on the outskirts of Alcalá de Henares. Tom's canopy had landed on his property, and, after the Air Force issued him a generous check, the *caballero* was as happy as a clam. In time, the whole thing blew over, so to speak.

Looking back more than forty years later, here's what I learned: (1) things can go to shit-in-a-hand-basket in a heartbeat, (2) I didn't enjoy being tossed around like a rag doll in a hurricane, (3) I'm still plagued by tinnitus at about 80 decibels, (4) I'm lucky there was a stick in the back seat of that *Phantom*, and (5) I'm grateful to all the great fighter pilots who gave me lots of stick time so I could spoil the Grim Reaper's plans that day.

Photo credit: depositphotos.com

A-6 *Intruder*

CHAPTER 23

ALONE

GENIUSES IN WASHINGTON prohibited bombing North Vietnam's only big steel plant -- Thai Nguyen – until 1967. By that time, the North Vietnamese had surrounded it with the most densely packed batteries of surface-to-air missiles (SAMs) and anti-aircraft guns (AAA) in history. Geniuses down the hall from the other geniuses decided to send eight Navy A-6 *Intruders* to shut Thai Nguyen down. Three in-flight refueling tankers and eight armed *Intruders* launched off the *USS Kitty Hawk* at three in the morning. Each attack A-6 was loaded with radar-jamming equipment and thirteen 1,000-pound bombs. Every enemy missile operator and gunner north of the DMZ licked his chops and waited.

Early in the mission, one A-6 turned back with a malfunctioning weapons system. Seven *Intruders* left. Moments later, a second A-6 aborted because it couldn't take on fuel from the tanker. Six *Intruders* left. As the strike force approached the North Vietnamese coastline, two more A-6s lost their weapons systems and had to return to the *Kittyhawk*. Four *Intruders* left. The remaining A-6s split into two elements flying 200 feet above the ground as they maneuvered to attack the steel plant from opposing directions. The number of guns and missiles waiting to pound the inbound attackers, while classified, was a large number. The only positive result of going from eight A-6s down to four was that it lowered the chances of a mid-air collision over the target.

Fifteen minutes to target: one of the A-6s lost its computer system and had to abort. Three *Intruders* left. Thirteen minutes to target: another A-6 lost its computer system and had to return to the carrier. Two *Intruders* left. Nine minutes to target: one of the two remaining A-6s lost its radar. Snaking through mountains at 200 feet above the ground in weather at night without radar wasn't the place for any mother's son. The electronically sightless *Intruder* returned to the *Kittyhawk*, leaving one lonely *Intruder*.

The solitary remaining A-6's chances of avoiding a mid-air were excellent. The lone A-6's chances of avoiding getting hosed, however, were horrendous. It crossed the initial point and began its run-in toward the steel mill's angry red furnaces like a dart headed for hell. Too low for SAMs to get a lock-on, the *Intruder* roared along in the dark at 540 knots barely 200 feet above the trees. North Vietnamese gunners sent thousands of rounds and tracers arching up just behind the *Intruder*. The jet popped up to 1,500 feet above the ground at ten miles from the target, giving every living gunner in the region a splendid opportunity to bag an A-6. Radar Homing and Warning sensors in the cockpit buzzed, chirped, rattled, and wailed. The night sky lit up with a salvo of 11 SAM launches. The pilot jinked like a wounded wombat to defeat the missiles. One missile overshot the *Intruder* and hit the ground. Triple-A riddled the plane with holes, but the *Intruder* flew on, and throughout the violent maneuvering, the A-6 maintained its lock on the steel plant. The *Intruder* pickled its bombs about 9,000 feet from the target and maneuvered low and fast toward the relative safety of the mountains northeast of Hanoi, up toward the buffer zone near the Chinese border. Change that "toward" to "into."

An Air Force surveillance plane, *Big Eye*, had a big mouth, too, and it broadcast a tad too enthusiastically, "Border Violation Red, Six Zero miles north of Bullseye," informing everyone with a rice hat, a radio, and a gun that a Yankee Sky Pirate was sneaking through the restricted zone. So the pilot flew a little faster ... and a little lower.

The lone *Intruder* put the steel plant's primary furnace out of action. The A-6 landed on the *Kittyhawk* with plenty of battle damage but all vital systems operating. The Grim Reaper had missed the best chance he might ever have to destroy the brave crew of the solitary *Intruder*.

Zimmerman, Richard. *There I was: Sea Stories from the United States Naval Academy Class of 1965*. Gateway Press, 2002.

Ross "Rosie" Detwiler

Bridgewater, Connecticut
United States Air Force Academy
Brigadier General, United States Air Force
F-100, F-4, T-37, O-2, C-5
Falcons 10-7X, Global Express,
Gulfstream II, III, IV
Chief Pilot, American Can Company,
Primerica, Travelers Group, Citigroup

CHAPTER 24

DON'T LOOK DOWN

A REALLY QUICK WAY to cash in your Grim Reaper chips in a supersonic jet was to gawk around inside the cockpit during a critical phase of flight like, say, dropping bombs down in the weeds. Looking down inside the cockpit close to the ground was as dimwitted as the modern-day malpractice of texting while driving a car.

Back in 1968 I was flying F-100 *Super Sabres* in the 416th Fighter Squadron out of Phù Cát, South Vietnam. Other than common sense, there was no actual law against looking around inside the cockpit on a low level bombing pass, but "peeking" while flying low and fast could kill you quicker than any text ever would. I learned that lesson the hard way on a hot June day north of Qui Nho'n, South Vietnam.

I was "Lieutenant Fuzz," a shiny new F-100 pilot. I had accumulated most of my 200 flying hours in the jet we affectionately called the *Hun* at "gun school" at Luke Air Force Base, Arizona. There were three other lieutenants like me flying in the 416th -- Marshall Clinkscales, Scotty Roberts, and Mike Sargent. (We teased "Lieutenant Sergeant" about his "government-issue" name, reminding him of Joseph Heller's creation Major Major in the novel *Catch 22*.)

In the history of the F-100 *Super Sabre*, 324 pilots eventually died in 889 accidents not attributed to enemy fire. Scotty Roberts became one of the fatalities during a low-altitude close air support mission during my first month at Phù Cát.

Photo credit: U.S. Air Force

Scotty fired his rockets okay, but, on his first low-angle bomb pass, he leveled off for a millisecond, pulled up too late, and hit the ground. His *Hun* skidded through rice paddies for a quarter of a mile before blowing up. In addition, the bomb he had just attempted to drop didn't explode. It was a dud. I didn't know the cause of Scotty's accident right away, but I *did* know that I had no intention of making the same mistake.

A week after Scotty went down, I was scheduled to fly *Elect Two-Two* on the wing of Major Jamie Jamieson in support of the 1st ROK (Republic of Korea) Tiger Division. The Koreans were fighting in the mountains near Phù Cát, and they needed air support badly. We were fragged to carry the same weapons load Scotty had carried – rockets and "snake," delivered in that order. We routinely selected "ARM" with the bomb arming switch down on the left side panel of the cockpit when we were within the target area at a safe altitude. Even though it wasn't required for firing rockets, we did this to preclude looking down into the cockpit at low altitude.

The procedure for firing rockets was to establish a 400-knot dive, fix the gun pipper on the target and, at a range of 3,000 feet, let 'er rip. The rockets launched in salvos off the outboard pylons, and, when they hit the target, it was like the Fourth of July!

"Snake" was the nickname for a 500-pound bomb with folding fins lashed to it. With the bomb arm switch in "ARM," pickling off a "snake" caused arming wires fixed to the aircraft to pull out of the nose fuse, tail fuse, and a band holding fins retracted against the sides of the bomb. When the band released, the fins flipped outward ninety degrees to form a shape like a parachute. The deployed fins slowed the bomb's air speed so we could get close to the target for accuracy and get enough separation from the explosion to prevent blowing ourselves out of the air. "Snake" was ideal for helping friendly forces in tight skirmishes with the enemy, and it saved a lot of American and allied lives.

As we rounded the Phù Cát mountains inbound to the target, Jamie switched to the forward air controller (FAC) UHF radio frequency and checked in with *Covey*, the call sign of a very brave man in a tiny O-1 *Bird Dog* observation aircraft. He was orbiting in the area to direct our fire to protect the Koreans from the enemy.

"*Covey*, this is *Elect Two-One* and *Two-Two*, Mission Two-one-zero-two, two F-100s with rockets and 'snake.' Twenty minutes of play time. Think I've got you … rock your wings."

Covey rocked the wings of his aircraft to provide positive identification. Jamie porpoised his jet as a signal to me to drop back in trail and he asked me whether I had sight of the FAC. I told him that I did. *Covey* radioed details of the target.

"*Elect Two-One* Flight, our troops are going to lob a Willie Pete (white phosphorous) mortar round to mark the target. Hit the smoke."

Covey went off air to coordinate with the ground troops on an FM radio frequency.

"O.K. they just fired the mortar," *Covey* said. "The friendlies are north of the smoke. Run in from east to west and pull up to the south over the top of the mountain. Got the smoke?"

"Lead's got the smoke."

"Two's got the smoke."

"Lead's in from the east."

"Two's in behind you, Lead. I'll fire after you pull up."

In the rush to set up for the rocket pass, I failed to select "ARM." My oversight had no effect on the rockets, but it would have a serious consequence when it was time to drop "snake." My rockets lit up the target.

"Good hits, *Elect Flight*. Okay, you're cleared to drop your 'snake' next."

We had to pull hard off the target to avoid slamming into rapidly rising mountains. Jamie turned back to the east, went feet wet over the South China Sea, and returned feet dry during his roll-in.

"Lead's in from the east."

I reached down into the cockpit and selected "BOMBS." I still hadn't selected "ARM." I was just rolling in when Jamie's first bomb detonated.

"Good hit, *Elect Two-One*," *Covey* said. "*Two* ... same hole."

"Two," I acknowledged.

I concentrated hard as I pressed in closer to the target. Airspeed was perfect. I put the pipper on the rear edge of Jamie's bomb crater. Pickle. "Thunk." The left inboard pylon shuddered. A sudden doubt – had I selected the

"ARM" position? I couldn't help it: I looked inside the cockpit ... located the armament panel ... found the bomb arm switch ....

When my eyes snapped back up, the canopy was filled with trees! I involuntarily screamed into my oxygen mask and instinctively pulled back hard on the stick. The *Hun* dug in. I thought I was dead. I didn't know how many *G*s I was pulling as the rising terrain slipped below me, but I cleared the peak of the mountain and miraculously, wondrously, I was alive!

Covey couldn't resist stating the obvious: "I thought you were gonna prang big time, *Two*." He wasn't the only one. And to top things off, I'd dropped a dud, an unarmed bomb!

Jamie and I finished dropping our remaining bombs. *Covey* gave us our battle damage assessment as I joined up with Lead. During my rejoin, I could see the burned-out foliage where Scotty Roberts had died.

By that time, I was fairly sure that I knew what had happened to Scotty. If I had tried to pull out a split second later than I did, I would have augured into the target just like he had.

We popped back over the hills to enter the pattern at Phù Cát in a sweeping right hand turn onto initial at 325 knots. Snap into the break. Right on altitude. All my senses were cooking at double time. Downwind turn to final at 190 knots, slowing to 172 knots plus fuel on final. Touch down. Nose down. Chute deployed. Alive.

After engine shutdown, I unbuckled my straps and tried to stand up, but my legs were shaking too much to support my weight. After a few seconds to calm the trembling, I grasped the edge of the canopy for leverage to get out of the cockpit and to step down the ladder.

Jamie was already sitting on the right side bench of the squadron "bread truck" when it stopped to pick me up.

"You figure there's any need for a lengthy debrief?" he asked.

"No, sir."

"Dumb-ass."

I felt a lot of emotions: grief for Scotty, joy at dodging the Reaper, and humility, knowing that sheer luck was the only reason I wasn't dead like Scotty. I had learned a hard lesson -- don't look down!

Brigadier General Ross Detwiler, United States Air Force (Retired), is the author of *The Great Muckrock and Rosie*. It is available on Amazon.

Photo courtesy of Everett Beasley

Skip "Polar Bear" Beasley

Nashville, Tennessee
Tulane University
Lieutenant Colonel, United States Air Force
F-4, F-5, F-16, Hawker *Hunter*,
BAe *Harrier*
BAe Jetstream, B-727, MD-10, MD-11
Corporate Express, Federal Express

CHAPTER 25

¡FUEGO!

ON JULY 31, 1992, Illinois Air National Guard Captain Donald "Lumpy" Lechrone of the 170th Fighter Squadron punched out of his single-engine F-16A *Falcon* after takeoff from Capital Airport near Springfield, Illinois for a flight to Denmark. During his ejection, Captain Lechrone was tragically killed by a piece of aircraft debris. I never had the pleasure of meeting Captain Lechrone, but I knew his airplane, tail number 82-0943, *real* well.

We pilots who flew the F-16 *Falcon* or, later, the F-16 *Fighting Falcon,* called it the F-16 *Viper.* This particular *Viper* and I went back a ways. Six years earlier, while assigned to the 401st Tactical Fighter Wing at Torrejón Air Base, Spain, *Viper 943* had developed a massive fuel leak on landing from the morning's sortie and was parked on the ramp in a puddle of fuel. To prevent blowing the entire ramp to Kingdom Come, a fire engine hosed down the spill. *Viper 943's* crew chief removed fuel that had pooled inside the fuselage and replaced a faulty fuel seal. He turned *Viper 943* over to me for my flight with Major Jim Donley and First Lieutenant Bill Manning. Our formation took off as a three-ship and headed southeast of Torrejón for a dog fight in LED 132, airspace reserved for air combat maneuvering.

During the third engagement, I broke into Bill with a full afterburner eight-*G* turn into the vertical that forced him to overshoot. I was blasting almost straight up, my airspeed decelerating through 220 knots, when I heard Bill on the radio shouting words no fighter jock wants to hear.

"Knock it off! Knock it off! *Three*, you're on fire."

The message was of great importance to me, because I was *Three*. I used to keep a list of acceptable ways to die, and being incinerated in a *Viper* wasn't one of them. Imagining myself imitating Haley's Comet, I pulled the throttle to idle and kicked in full rudder to get my nose down and gain airspeed. While in the side slip I glanced back so I could see the long trail of fire streaming out from the rear end of my *Viper*. (Bill's gun camera film later showed that the spectacular fire trail was longer than a football field.) Suspecting a massive fuel leak like the one that had occurred earlier in the day, I pointed the nose of the jet straight down in an attempt to put out the fire. It didn't work right away. The flight manual advised ejection if fire persisted. The fire was approaching my definition of "persisting," but I was reluctant to jump out of my $20 million *Viper*. Forty seconds after the fire started, Jim and Bill reported that the flames were out. Jim joined up on my wing and described the damage to my afterburner as looking like someone had used a chain saw to cut away five feet of the "turkey feathers" section of my afterburner nozzles. Fully expecting the engine to quit at any moment, I set the throttle at eighty per cent and turned the *Viper* toward Albacete's Los Llanos Air Base, a Spanish Air Force *Mirage* F1 base that our squadron used as an emergency divert field. *Picasso* (the Spanish Ground Control Intercept unit) launched a precautionary Spanish Air Force search-and-rescue mission. Jim told Bill to return to Torrejón. As Jim escorted me toward Los Llanos, I prayed that my jet wouldn't light off like a firecracker again and, when my prayers allowed, I mentally reviewed dead-stick landing procedures.

I declared an emergency on Los Llanos Tower frequency. The controller was an excitable fellow, and he sputtered a long reply, regrettably, in Spanish. My mastery of the Spanish language was, to be euphemistic, limited. I inventoried my Spanish vocabulary: *vino, cerveza, fuego* ... that's it ... *fuego*! Fire!

"*¡Fuego! ¡Fuego! ¡Fuego!*" I said slowly, hoping to calm down the controller. "I will land to the west." Landing to the west would give me a headwind so I could get the *Viper* stopped before I added to the day's excitement by running off the end of the runway.

This time, the controller said only one word.

"Roger." (It sounded like "Rah-yer.")

I was grateful that the engine kept running at idle power, but, as a precaution, I performed a simulated flameout landing starting overhead the Los Llanos runway at eight thousand feet. I landed uneventfully and turned off at the end of the runway into the bomb de-arming area where I was surrounded by a convention of fire trucks. I shut down the engine and emergency-egressed the cockpit with as much dignity as I could master to disguise my hammering heart and twitching nerve endings. (It wouldn't do to show trepidation in front of our Spanish allies.) At the Fire Chief's gestured invitation, I jumped down onto his truck. Three fire engines doused the tail end of the *Viper*.

Things were starting to settle down when I spotted a staff car approaching with a flag on the hood. The fire fighters snapped to attention.

"*¿Es El Jefe?*" I asked. (I wanted to know whether this was the Los Llanos wing commander.)

"*¡Si, si! ¡Es El Jefe!*" a fire fighter replied.

I snapped to attention and saluted the handsome Spanish Colonel who was walking toward me. He stopped in front of me.

"Skip?" (It sounded like "Skeep.")

"Yago?" I said.

El Jefe was Colonel Yago Bobadilla. As a captain Spanish Exchange Officer, he had been my flight instructor during F-4 *Phantom* training at Luke Air Force Base, Arizona 14 years earlier. He gave me a bear hug. One of the fire fighters commented that Colonel Bobadilla was so famous that he knew all the American fighter pilots.

Full disclosure requires that I admit that I forgot to call the Torrejón Command Post to let them know that I hadn't died on the Plains of La Mancha. I didn't think of calling "Mom" until I was two hours into drinking Bobadilla Gran Reserve Brandy in celebration of my reunion with Yago and his wife. By then I was slurring. Figuring that the clever lads in the Command Post would have deduced that I had made it when Jim returned to Torrejón in one piece, I delayed making the call for quite a while.

The United States Air Forces in Europe presented Jim and me with airmanship and in-flight leadership awards for saving the *Viper* that day. Based on the findings of an incident board, an inspection of all Air Force F-16s revealed that a number of afterburner nozzle control mechanisms had manufacturing flaws.

I don't know why *Viper 943* went down six years later, but I've often wished that the good fortune I experienced with that airplane had extended to Captain Donald "Lumpy" Lechrone of the Illinois Air National Guard. He was a legend among the great "Boyz from Illinoiz."

Photo courtesy of Jim Strawn

James Edward (Jim) Strawn

Radford, Virginia
Armstrong State College
Virginia Commonwealth University
Lt. Col., United States Marine Corps
C-152, C-172, T-34, T-28, T-1A, F9F-8,
F8U, TA4-F, F-4B, OV10, UH-34, C-17

CHAPTER 26

EJECT

SOME COMMENTATORS have called the F-8 *Crusader* the most beautiful fighter ever built. That certainly was my opinion. Ignoring for a moment the sleek lines and proportions of the *Crusader*, I even admired its marvelous components.

The wings had just the right taper. They were low on drag and high on versatility. They could slice through thick air at sea level like a razor blade through water, but they could also suspend the *Crusader* at high angles of attack and low indicated airspeeds at the edge of space.

The Pratt & Whitney J57 engine slammed me back in my seat as the engine and catapult tossed me like a dart out over the ocean, powering me just above the waves or thrusting me up to the zone where the sky turned black.

Even the hook was a marvel. An innocuous piece of chromium-vanadium steel I generally took for granted until I needed it. Then, in about a second, it could absorb the stress of over 20,000 pounds landing at over 120 knots to bring a *Crusader* to a halt on the deck of a carrier.

I took the canopy for granted, too. I could see right through it, yet it cocooned me from thermal extremes of 150 blazing degrees on a runway at Yuma, Arizona and, three minutes later, seventy below zero at 50,000 feet. A bird strike that would rip my head off simply vaporized into a gazillion fragments against the *Crusader's* marvelous canopy. The canopy was my shield against the Grim Reaper, my womb of safety … until it wasn't.

Location: Marine Corps Air Station Beaufort, South Carolina. I wasn't even supposed to fly on the day the Grim Reaper came to collect me. I was a First Lieutenant with 700 flight hours, most of which was in the F-8U2. I was the assigned Squadron Duty Officer (SDO) for Marine Fighter Squadron VMF-333 for the day. After a busy morning, I took time for lunch. I ate one of the best BLTs I've ever tasted. It was almost the *last* BLT I ever tasted.

Following my repast, I returned to the squadron. The Operations Officer had assigned my good friend First Lieutenant Tom Fraser to relieve me of SDO duty so I could suit up and stand by to fly in the Ready Room. When I got scrambled, I saddled into my *Crusader*, and launched – afterburner blazing -- to join up with my flight leader, First Lieutenant Joe McDonald, who was headed for the Atlantic Ocean on vectors for a supersonic intercept of simulated intruders. Joe was established at Mach 1.4 at 34,000 feet, so I had to push it up to Mach 1.55 to join him for the intercept. That's when the Reaper struck.

Ear-splitting noise … overpowering sub-freezing windblast … glass fragments flying everywhere. My canopy shattered into a billion pieces. I attempted to lean forward for protection from the terrible force of 600 knots of wind. I pulled the throttle back to slow down. I reached up to raise my helmet visor in an attempt to see better, but my visor had been ripped away by the wind. I was being flash-frozen at fifty degrees below zero. I had to slow down to survive, so I pulled the throttle all the way back and deployed the speed brakes. Then, five seconds after the implosion of my canopy, the wind blast pulled my ejection seat face curtain enough to initiate the ejection sequence. I was shot out of the cockpit into a supersonic tumble that contorted my body so violently that I caught a glimpse of the bottoms of my flying boots.

Images were fleeting. My helmet was almost torn off my head. My arms and legs flailed wildly. Extreme wind forces shredded the stabilizer drogue chute, so my ejection seat kept tumbling violently until I separated from it. I had to remove my helmet to inspect my parachute, which had only partially deployed. The risers were tangled and I had only three-quarters of a canopy. While I was hurtling toward the ground, my *Crusader* was still flying faster than the speed of sound. (I later learned that it crashed 55 miles away on the Fort Jackson artillery range.)

Because I was descending over farmland, I jettisoned the life raft so I wouldn't land on it and do myself even more harm. Fortunately, I think, I hit the ground going backwards. I released the parachute Koch fittings and lay still for a moment.

A farm kid playing nearby had watched my dramatic arrival to his doorstep in wonder. I told him to make an emergency telephone call. His eyes were as big as frisbees because mangled Marines in *G*-suits didn't routinely plop down from the sky onto his yard. Who knows how big *my* eyes were. I lay there, battered and bruised, way outside my comfort zone.

An Air Force helicopter arrived about 45 minutes after my less-than-textbook parachute landing fall. I could have used a gallon or so of morphine, but the flight surgeon on the chopper wasn't serving any. He busied himself splinting my legs on the way to the Shaw Air Force Base Hospital.

Inside the hospital, a second flight surgeon informed me that my left shoulder was separated. He was a sturdy, hands-on kind of guy who grabbed my left arm, shoved a foot against my arm pit, and started pulling like he was in a tug-of-war. (It's worth noting here that Marine fighter pilots call

Navy enlisted corpsmen "Doc" and medical officers "Quack.") Finally (and mercifully) he gave up and told me that they could fix my shoulder later on when they fixed my legs. Then, thank God, they put me to sleep.

It took seven months to recover from surgeries on my knees and left shoulder. Rehabilitation was unpleasant, but it got me back on flying status. Despite my most positive thinking, I secretly feared that, if I ever had to punch out again, my legs from the knees down would go flying off into space. I wasn't keen on the first supersonic run I had to make during my work-up a year later for my deployment to Vietnam. I had become the first F-8 pilot to survive a supersonic ejection. I didn't want to become the second. As it turned out, I soon forgot all my concerns about canopies so I could focus on North Vietnamese and Viet Cong AAA gunners who were doing their level best to blow me out of the sky.

Truly, the F-8 *Crusader* was a fantastic creation of synergistic components. However clumsily, my F-8's Martin-Baker ejection seat blasted me out of the Grim Reaper's grasp the day my canopy disintegrated. Although ejection seats manufactured by Martin-Baker have saved the lives of almost 8,000 other pilots over the past 70 years, the pain in my legs and shoulder to this day remind me that I would be remiss if I didn't recommend employing it at speeds as much below 1,000 miles an hour as possible.

Jim Strawn's incredible survival story first appeared in Ron Knott's book *Supersonic Cowboys*.

Photo courtesy of Wade Price

Wade Price

Fairfax Station, Virginia
George Mason University
1st Lieutenant, United States Air Force Reserve
T-6 *Texan*, T-1 *Jayhawk*, C-17 *Globemaster III*
CFI, Manassas Regional Airport

CHAPTER 27

COMPLACENCY

THE GRIM REAPER, a particularly promiscuous predator, wants to bag pilots, and he doesn't care if they're old or young, smart or stupid. He's got a zillion ways to fill his quota, as Wade Price discovered one beautiful, still, and terrifying late afternoon in Northern Virginia.

After college I worked full-time as a flight instructor for 18 months. Most of my students were semi-retired, middle-aged men looking for a challenging hobby. Many of them had built impressive careers, but their skill sets didn't include three-dimensional spatial orientation, so it was my job to teach these old dogs new tricks. A procession of well-meaning but ham-handed business executives scared me with the unexpected just often enough to keep me on my toes. I dreamed of having just one relaxing flight that didn't require me to be on guard every second.

My dream came true one summer afternoon when, a Marine Captain, an EA-6B *Prowler* Pilot, showed up in civilian clothes wanting to get checked-out in a small plane so he could take his family flying. Of course, I was delighted to fly with a professional military aviator.

Recently, I had been selected to fly Air Force Reserve C-17 *Globemaster III*s, so I spent a lot of the briefing time asking him about military flying. He was happy to answer my questions, but he was most interested in learning about our training aircraft, a 1975 AA-5B Grumman *Tiger*. I assumed that, compared to the complex *Prowler* he routinely flew, flying the little *Tiger* was going to be a piece of cake for him.

Out in the practice area, I asked the Marine to warm up by demonstrating a few steep turns and stalls. It was a standard way to begin any lesson. He flew just fine. If he seemed a little out of his comfort zone, I was sure he'd get over it when he had spent a couple of hours in the *Tiger*. After completing our air work, we flew to the Culpeper Airport traffic pattern for some landings.

Usually, I demonstrated the first landing, and I was tempted to let my ego out of the corral by laying down a perfect approach and landing, but humility prevailed. I figured that, if the Marine could land a $40-million combat jet weighing over 30,000 pounds on the pitching deck of an aircraft carrier at night, he could certainly land a little 2,000-pound *Tiger* on an immovable asphalt runway in calm winds in the daytime.

I talked him through each leg of the pattern, providing him with target speeds and power settings. I admit that I was complacent. I was so enamored of his experience that I wasn't even guarding the flight controls. I noticed that his hands were clamped onto the yoke and he was perspiring slightly, but his approach to the runway was stable. I tried to imagine my first approach to a carrier in his A-6: I'd be choking the stick like a monkey bar over the Grand Canyon. Things were going so well. Suddenly, things weren't going well at all.

The Marine slipped a touch low on short final, not enough to incite panic, but enough to warrant debriefing. Things then went south faster than a goosed greyhound. I was suddenly suspended in my seat belt as though cresting a hill on a roller coaster. The horizon disappeared up over my head and I was staring straight down at the huge white "4" painted on the approach end of the runway. It was a real big "4," and it was getting bigger at a rapid rate.

I instinctively yanked the yoke back into my gut like my life depended on it (which it did). I felt the nose wheel slam onto the runway, quickly followed by the main gear. We bounded back up into the air like a kid vaulting off a trampoline. The Marine pushed the throttle to the firewall and yelled.

"Go around!" Four times.

I heard him the first time. With my right hand still clamped onto the yoke, I reached for the throttle with my left hand. He pulled his right hand away from the throttle and said, with military precision, "Your aircraft!"

The propeller appeared to be undamaged, which was a marvel. The RPM gauge was stable. I counted the wings, and there were still two of them. I wasn't complacent anymore. I felt the way President Lincoln might have felt if John Wilkes Booth had missed – happy to be alive, but edgy. I asked the Marine what had happened. He couldn't explain, but he made up for it by apologizing a lot. I got him back on the controls and talked him through some more landings. Thankfully, for the sake of my heart, they were uneventful. Compared to most pilots flying the *Tiger* for the first time, the Marine's landings were really quite good. Compared to his own first attempt, the rest of his landings were fabulous.

Back on the ground at the Manassas Airport, I examined the propeller for signs of damage. By some phenomenal exception to the laws of geometry and physics, the prop was fine. I signed the Marine off so he could rent a plane. He tried to overpay me for my time, but I politely refused. A man is seldom as generous as during the lull immediately following an encounter with the Reaper. The gift of life was sufficient payment. Afterwards, I tried to analyze how my brother had almost become an only child.

I routinely swapped seats in the *Tiger* so I was used to switching from left-hand-on-the-throttle to right-hand-on-the-throttle. That familiarity kept me from figuring out the cause of the incident. The Marine, however, *did* break the code. Two days after my dust-up with the Grim Reaper, the Marine sent me an email containing another apology and a reasonable explanation. For years he had flown jets exclusively with his right hand on the stick and his left hand on the throttles. When slipping below glide slope while flying a jet with a constant angle-of-attack on final, the action for correcting up to glide slope was to push his left hand forward. On the day of our training flight in the *Tiger*, his left hand had controlled the elevator (not the power). So, when the *Tiger* had descended too low on the glide slope as we crossed the threshold, his instinct – formed by years of habit – was to shove his left hand forward. Left hand forward in a *Prowler* meant more power. Left hand forward in the left seat of a *Tiger* meant a windscreen full of asphalt.

Unfortunately, flying with a skilled jet aviator had lured me into complacency. I had almost proved the axiom that "a low and slow airplane is just fast enough to barely kill you." Fortunately, the Reaper went off empty-handed and I learned from the experience.

Joe Boyles

Madison, Florida
United States Air Force Academy
Colonel, United States Air Force
F-4 *Phantom*

CHAPTER 28

OOPS

PILOTS AT KORAT Royal Thai Air Force Base were routinely directed to bomb a list of enemy targets like bridges, convoys, gun emplacements, and SAM sites. Bombing the Korat runway, however, was nowhere to be found on the target list. Unfortunately, that's exactly what Charlie Cox and Joe Boyles did in June of 1972. To be fair, the bombing wasn't intentional.

Cox and Boyles were members of the 35th Tactical Fighter Squadron "Pantons," one of the oldest fighter squadrons in the United States Air Force, dating back to 1917 when it was organized as the 35th Aero Squadron. They were scheduled to fly their F-4D *Phantom* as number three in *Gator* flight as a part of a Linebacker strike package against the Thai Nguyen steel factory located northwest of Hanoi. Each of the four *Phantoms* was loaded with a dozen 500-pound bombs carried on multiple ejector racks (MERs) attached to outboard wing pylons designated stations one and nine.

The four *Phantoms* in *Gator* flight were loaded to the maximum gross weight of 58,000 pounds. The bombs loaded on the outboard stations caused the center of gravity to move forward to such a degree that nose wheel liftoff speed and takeoff speed both occurred at 185 knots. Even with full afterburner, it took a lot of runway to get up to 185 knots at maximum gross weight, so most of Korat's 10,000-foot strip was behind *Gator Three* when Cox and Boyles lifted off. A "max-gross-takeoff" wasn't dull in the best of times, and, when *Gator Three's* main landing gear struts extended, things happened in a hurry.

First, a quick word about stray voltage. In a house with old wire and crumbling insulation, electric lights and motors have been known to turn on and off randomly. Such a house might be called "haunted." In a typical F-4D (a fighter plane fittingly named *Phantom)*, age, corrosion, gravity forces, twisting, turning, flexing, heat expansion, and cold contraction played hell with wire bundles that extended like a circulatory system throughout the aircraft. Insulation cracked and frayed over time, so "electrons" wandered around on paths where they weren't designed to travel. Stuff happened without pilot inputs from time to time, but the term "haunted" was seldom used.

Gator Three's nose gear strut extended to its full length, the nose wheels lifted off the ground, and the main landing gear struts extended as the wings reached flying speed and took over the job of supporting the aircraft. That's when stray voltage somehow energized the jettison circuits on the *Phantom's* outboard stations. Both MERs loaded with bombs separated from the pylons and fell to the runway.

Oblivious to the inferno their airplane had deposited on the departure end of the Korat runway, the crew of *Gator Three* marveled at the power of their F-4D. More than 6,000 pounds lighter in an instant, the *Phantom* accelerated like a scalded-ass ape. *Gator Three* closed on *Gator One* and *Two* for the rejoin faster, in the words of one historian, than a leopard running down a dik-dik.

Unable to observe the underside of their wings, Cox and Boyles commented on the excellence of their rejoin, completely unaware of the absence of stores on stations one and nine and blissfully ignorant of the legacy of explosions and raging fires they had left behind at Korat. A familiar voice addressed Cox and Boyles on the radio.

"*Gator Three*, this is *Four*. You lost all your bombs on takeoff."

Gator Lead, Squadron Commander Lyle "Sky King" Beckers, took one look at *Gator Three* and saw that both MERs full of bombs had gone walkabout. Beckers cleared *Gator Three* to return to Korat, because a *Phantom* without bombs over North Vietnam was about as useful as a pogo stick to a kangaroo. Flying unarmed over North Vietnam was operating at the wrong end of the risk/reward chart and was best left to photo reconnaissance pilots who made a living out of getting shot at that way.

Cox radioed *Fort Apache*, the Korat Command Post, to coordinate the return of *Gator Three* to land.

"Negative, negative, *Gator Three*!" a voice powered by too much coffee replied. "The Korat runway's been bombed and the runway's closed. Divert to another base!"

Instead of diverting, Cox persuaded *Fort Apache* to allow *Gator Three* to hold for an hour to burn off excess fuel while the Korat runway was cleared. Landing at their home base allowed immediate aircraft impoundment and an inspection that would hopefully exonerate the crew from the slightest culpability.

Only three of the 12 bombs had cooked off in low-order detonations, so Korat didn't become another Nagasaki. Two aircraft had been damaged, but no people had been injured. Nevertheless, everyone agreed that it was just as well that such unexpected conflagrations weren't common events.

Gator Four, who had been lumbering down the runway when the horizon ahead of his jet had turned into a fireball, had a different story to tell. In a display of exceptional agility by a bomb-laden *Phantom*, the pilot of *Gator Four* had

185

steered toward the extreme edge of the runway and had deftly avoided adding to the fireworks. The Thai Nguyen steel plant was a dangerous environment, but, to *Gator Four's* thinking, not terribly more so than his takeoff run through flames and debris.

Stray voltage was like a ghost: in one moment you could see it and, in the next moment, not. Maintenance couldn't trace the cause of the stray voltage, but the offending *Phantom* was sent back to Korea. Cox and Boyles were completely cleared of any lingering doubts when a crew back in Korea lifted off and promptly jettisoned wing fuel tanks loaded on stations one and nine. Stray voltage had struck again!

Despite the notoriety of bombing their own runway, Cox and Boyles could be grateful that the bomb-laden MERs had jettisoned symmetrically. Had it been otherwise, they likely would have experienced a fatal dose of extreme heat and terminal trauma and the Grim Reaper would have had a banner day.

Boyles, Joe. "The Tale of Gator Three." Richard Keyt's Internet web site -- https://www.keytlaw.com/f-4/gator-3/.

Photo courtesy of Karen Lee

Karen Lee

Taos, New Mexico
Embry Riddle Aeronautical University
C-46, Lear 35, B-727, B-747, DC-8
Trans World Airlines
Seaboard World Airlines
Orion Air
United Parcel Service

CHAPTER 29

BLUE SIDE UP

THE GRIM REAPER is a caricature to me now that I've logged thousands of hours flying B-747s around the world to places I couldn't even find on a map when I was a teenager.

Take me back to my start in aviation, however, when an engine failure lurked behind every turn and when vertigo lay in ambush inside every cloud, and the Reaper seemed a grimly real malevolent force.

I still remember flying in the Reaper's shadow on a day when turbulence, blowing snow, and vertigo tumbled my equilibrium and shook my confidence like never before.

On a forbidding, snowy day in Northern New Jersey, speculation about a missing plane was buzzing around the fixed base operation among my posse of inexperienced private pilots. Witnesses had reported a plane crash near a ridgeline north of the airport. The only plane missing from the ramp was a Cessna rented by a newly certificated private pilot named Mandrake Saltington.

For self-evident reasons, everyone called Mandrake, a big-boned 270-pounder, by his nickname, "Big Salty." Four hours had elapsed since Big Salty had taken off into cloudy skies speckled with snow flurries. Our imaginations ran wild when word came in about a plane crash near a ridgeline north of the airport. We imagined Big Salty's corpse pinned inside a crumpled Cessna or, only slightly less morbidly, we visualized Big Salty wandering around in shock -- traumatized and freezing -- through the woods. We had to act fast to find Big Salty before sunset.

We had four airplanes available to start the grid search. The boss designated a volunteer observer to assist each pilot. My assigned observer was Brandy, a woman almost twice my age. Brandy was an airport groupie and a single mother with a keen eye for potential husband material. Presumably because her legs were irresistible, she routinely highlighted them by wearing shorts year-round like a uniform. They were short-shorts, really.

Flying with me was an unfortunate turn of events for Brandy, because the latest love of her life was an overly-confident student pilot flying one of the other airplanes. The name of this self-professed gift to aviation and, indeed, self-professed gift to the entire female sex, was Crockett. (Did his parents not know that this was Northern Jersey, not the Alamo?) Crockett had a girl-pick-up-line a nautical mile long. Anyway, Brandy's body was in my plane, but her mind was in Crockett's. Having Brandy in my plane was unfortunate for me, too; her perfume made me want to puke.

Judging from Brandy's enthusiasm for Crockett, I was pretty sure that he had embellished his aviation prospects by suggesting to Brandy that, any day now, he might become a seven-forty-seven captain hauling in wads of cash. As I prepared to start my engine, all Brandy could talk about was her future with Crockett. After I cranked the engine and prepared to taxi out, I noticed that Brandy, my observer, was observing nothing but herself. She inspected her hair and lipstick in a compact mirror shaped like an oyster.

Brandy had reported for volunteer duty on this winter day wearing woolen mini-shorts on top of leggings. It was a fantastic look, if that was your thing. (I didn't know they made shorts out of wool.) I pondered whether the term "woolen shorts" was an oxymoron like "jumbo shrimp" or "open secret" or "conspicuously absent" (which Big Salty was) or "crash landing" (one of which Big Salty apparently had made).

Brandy was terribly mistaken if she thought the combination of cigarette smoke and her perfume would advance her journey along the path toward matrimony. The mixture was awful. The cockpit of a Cessna 172 wasn't big enough for me and Brandy. Nevertheless, being a team player, I explained the grid search method to her. I could tell that she wasn't really listening until I summarized.

"Big Salty could die if we don't find him before sundown."

"This is life or death!" she said.

"Yes, it is."

So, during the flight, Brandy put her lipstick away and earnestly strained to spot a white crumpled airplane wing sticking out of a snow bank. She diligently scanned the terrain below us as I flew our assigned grid. Back and forth. North and south. The winds were blustery out of the west, so I had to crab the airplane to maintain the proper ground track. Wind spilling over the ridgeline made for a bumpy ride, but it wasn't the bumps that made me feel sick. I almost gagged because of the stench of cigarettes and perfume. Brandy remained blissfully ignorant of my vulnerability.

I contemplated lots of internal questions as we bumped along through intermittent snow showers. I climbed to clear the ridge by just a couple of hundred feet. What if visibility dropped below a mile? What if my carburetor started icing up? What if my engine quit? Did I have enough fuel to get back to the airport? Could I tolerate that perfume for one minute longer?

As we approached the point where I'd have to climb again to clear the ridge, we entered a cloud. It was a white-out worse than the Russian steppe scene in the *Doctor Zhivago* movie. It was whiter than white. Miniature snowflakes committed suicide against the windscreen. Brandy uttered an oath. For the first time all day, we were on the same page.

From the moment we entered the milk bowl, my sense of balance was totally screwed up. I was dancing a *pasodoble* with vertigo. At one moment I felt like we were in a screaming death spiral. In the next moment, my inner ear convinced me we were about to stall. I was acutely aware of the approaching ridgeline, rocky and unforgiving. I glanced at Brandy's ashen face, the sight of which did nothing to relieve my spatial disorientation. I willed my head not to oscillate like a bobble-head doll. I had to remain calm and stationary for Brandy's sake. She was an adult, at least chronologically. She was an innocent adult depending on me. Oddly, I actually wanted to please her. I realized that somebody in that airplane had to get oriented quickly or Big Salty was going to have a couple of sidekicks. Somebody was going to have to fly that Cessna 172 out of this mess, and it wasn't going to be Perfume Girl.

My eyes darted around at a dozen objects – vertical velocity indicator, airspeed indicator, horizontal situation indicator, gyro horizon/attitude indicator, brown on the bottom and blue on the top. Thank God, training trumped panic. No matter how tumbled my spatial orientation was, I had to keep the blue side up. Surely we were close to the ridgeline. I focused on the instruments and fought to ignore what my sense of equilibrium was telling me. I rolled into a thirty-degree turn. Blue side up. I added power. We climbed. Blue side up.

When we popped up out of the snow shower, the sky above was deliciously blue. The afternoon sun was brilliant. The air was smooth. My head no longer felt as though it would topple off my shoulders. My symptoms of vertigo were gone. The horizon I observed out the window matched the perception of a horizon in my brain. I was spatially oriented again.

The radio crackled, and a voice announced that Big Salty was alive and had checked in by telephone. I later learned that, after his crash, he had hiked through the snowy woods to a ski cabin. Unaccustomed to beefy airmen in distress, an astonished European lady vacationing in the cabin had suitably bandaged the gash on his head. In the absence of a pharmacy, she also had given him a cup of coffee and a bottle of Paracetamol. Before the lady could caution him that the Tylenol-like European pain medication was a suppository, Big Salty had tossed two of the capsules down the hatch, chasing them with a manly gulp of coffee.

When my boss learned that Big Salty was safe and, presumably, pain-free, the search for Big Salty was called off. I aimed the airplane back toward home. Color had returned to Brandy's face. She was jabbering about her destiny with Crockett, deliriously happy about her pending role, however delusional, as a "Mrs. Captain."

I didn't mind. I was contented to have fought off the worst case of vertigo I'd ever encountered. I wondered whether Brandy had sensed anything amiss. It turned out that she had.

"Were you scared?" she asked.

"You?" I saw no need for a full confession.

"Nope," she said. "Once your head stopped bobbing around, I figured you had it under control." She was more likeable when she wasn't babbling about Crockett. "I've seen you when the crap hits, and you're calmer than the rest of those schmucks." That was high praise from Brandy. She sighed. "You did good."

Good enough to ignore every sensory message in my body. Good enough to refuse to panic. Good enough to fly out of the shadow of the Grim Reaper. Good enough to keep the blue side up.

Notwithstanding her woolen shorts, dreadful perfume, and dubious choice of boyfriends, Brandy, I decided, was okay.

Photo courtesy of Lenny Johnson

Lenny "Squirrel" Johnson

Wolfeboro, New Hampshire
Bowdoin College
Captain, United States Navy
F-8, F-4
B-727, B-737, B-747, B-777, DC-8, DC-10
United Airlines

CHAPTER 30

J-57

THE REAPER COULD BAG YOU in a lot of ways over North Vietnam. Some were quick and painless. Others were excruciatingly painful and went on for years before the end came. Few locations in history have been as heavily protected by anti-aircraft weapons as a stretch along the Red River. During 1966 I flew into the zone almost daily, flying photo reconnaissance missions in the RF-8 *Crusader* off the *USS Hancock.*

In retrospect, it was the most enjoyable flying of my long aviation career. It was challenging, exciting, scary, exhilarating, and beautiful -- never boring. Crossing the coast outbound, mission complete, headed home to the *Hancock,* a hot shower, and dinner was a great feeling -- good for another day. But the good feeling didn't last long, because, after dinner, planning for the next day's mission began. The six months of intense flying on Yankee Station wasn't nearly as enjoyable at the time as it would seem in retrospect. I remember anticipating going home to San Diego a lot more than the next day's mission over Hanoi.

To obtain the best photo resolution, we had to fly below 5,000 feet, which made our *Crusaders* extremely vulnerable. Our only defense was to keep the aircraft constantly moving about the sky -- changing altitude and direction. We also kept the speed up around 600 knots. The scary part came when I had to maintain constant speed, altitude, and heading over the target. That was also the time I had my head in the cockpit to adjust film speed and position. (Maybe not seeing the AAA bursts going off around me was a good thing.)

We often photographed targets before and after they were hit. Of course, the Vietnamese gunners knew to expect us shortly after a strike, so their geometry problem had a simple solution: they would simply fill the block of air we had to fly through with lead and exploding devices. The hostile environment took its toll. The squadron started the tradition of planting a pine tree next to the eighteenth tee at our home base golf course every time we lost a pilot, which happened way too often. In just a few years, a beautiful stand of pines grew to surround the tee box on an otherwise barren Miramar desert course.

On the way to Haiphong on the day of my story, my wingman notified me of fluid streaking along the belly of my *Crusader*. The F-8 was a notorious "leaker." My gauges were all normal, so I dismissed it. I was a new replacement pilot, and I wanted to impress. I certainly wasn't going to use a hydraulic leak as an excuse to abort. We pressed on into the harbor, descending to fifty feet over the decks of Russian ships delivering anti-aircraft missiles to the North Vietnamese. Our wing tips skimmed just above the waves as we weaved between craggy karst islands at just below the speed of sound. My wingman and I had almost reached the pop up point when my engine warning light illuminated. My oil quantity gauge was pegged on zero, which solved the mystery of the stream of fluid on the belly of my plane. The lifeblood of my J-57 engine had bled out, leaving me with no choice but to turn toward the *Hancock* and to prepare to eject.

The J-57 was such a great engine that it had been chosen to power not only the F-8, but bombers like the B-52

Stratofortress and B-57 *Canberra* and fighters like the F-100 *Super Sabre*, F-101 *Voodoo*, and the F-102 *Delta Dagger*. No matter how good the engine was, however, it needed oil to run. The flight manual advised that, without oil, I had up to 15 minutes of running time by setting the throttle at 86% of power. That was enough time to get me halfway to the *Hancock*.

I dutifully prepared for ejection by stowing my gear, lowering the seat, checking my equipment, and mentally rehearsing parachute and life raft procedures I had practiced back in San Diego harbor. Fifteen minutes came and went. My gutsy J-57 was still running smoothly.

The Captain of the *Hancock* decided to risk taking me aboard. He turned the ship into the wind and ordered an emergency pull-forward of aircraft to clear the landing area on the carrier deck. I hadn't considered bringing this hurting bird aboard; as a result, the ship was ready for me before I was ready for the ship. I was high, fast, and still dumping fuel to get my gross weight down below the maximum for landing. Leaving the throttle at 86% wasn't helping me get down or to decelerate to be in the optimum position for a carrier landing.

I had been running without oil for about thirty-five minutes. That beautiful engine kept on chugging far beyond its predicted life expectancy. One thing I never thought about during my attempt to get aboard was that the ejection seat I was riding on wouldn't save me below 1,000 feet on final with a 700 feet per minute sink rate. My parachute wouldn't have time to blossom before I hit the water at 160 knots. I should have insisted on a controlled ejection alongside the ship rather than trying to bring it aboard, but being the inexperienced (one could rightly say "dumb") kid that I was, I acquiesced to the Captain's order.

The Landing Signal Officer (LSO) would normally have waved me off, but he knew that my first approach was probably my only shot, so he let me continue. I hit the landing area, but my *Crusader's* excess speed lowered the fuselage angle and caused the tail hook to jump over the arresting wire. It was normal to go to full throttle when hitting the deck in case of a bolter, but I hesitated. I boltered off the angle deck and the plane began to shake as it approached a stall. I had no choice but to shove the throttle full forward. Amazingly, the engine responded and powered me to downwind for another try. Again, the prudent thing for me to have done was to eject on downwind while I had the chance to do so safely, but I was angry at myself for blowing my chance at getting aboard. I was thinking about having to explain to my boss and the accident board why I had boltered.

I was flying on borrowed time. I knew I was asking too much of this engine. I turned onto final and called "*Crusader* ball." This time I was on-speed and on-glide slope. Everything went perfectly. I "trapped" and the Air Boss radioed for me to shut down right there, so I could be towed out of the way as soon as possible. I had taken up too much of his precious deck time. He had 20 planes waiting to launch and a recovery to follow.

Before I had even climbed out of the cockpit, a mechanic crawled down the intake to inspect the engine. I was grateful to have my feet firmly planted on deck when he reported that the engine had seized. Wow! That Pratt & Whitney J57 had exceeded all expectations. It had kept running for forty minutes without oil, including a big throttle change to full power near the end, waiting until I was safely aboard before dying. I thank the Lord for the miracle that got me home that day.

For an in-depth version of Len Johnson's missions over North Vietnam, read Ron Knott's *Supersonic Cowboys*.

Photo credit: rkc359/depositphotos.com

Ravens

Hank Allen
Charles "Bing" Ballou
Mike Cavanaugh
Sam Deichelman
Craig Duehring
Charles "Chuck" Engle
Dick Ezinga
Fred "Cowboy" Platt
Ron "Papa Fox" Rinehart
Tom Shera
Marlin Siegwalt

CHAPTER 31

GOLDEN BB

THE RANDOMNESS of the Grim Reaper's carnage is reflected in the term "Golden BB." It connotes a single bullet taking a victim's life as though predetermined by fate. No logic. No reason. Golden BBs show no regard for an aircraft's type, altitude, or speed or for a pilot's physical attributes, flying record, rank, or reputation. The arbitrary nature of Golden BBs was on vivid display among the *Ravens*, a secret group of highly-vetted fighter pilots who wore civilian clothes while flying unmarked O-1 *Bird Dogs* to direct air strikes against communist targets in Laos from 1966 to 1973. Longevity wasn't a *Raven* perk. One of every six *Raven* pilots was killed in action, often by a Golden BB.

Marlin Siegwalt's tour as a *Raven* was near an end. In seven days he could leave the primitive and dangerous environment of Laos for an assignment back in the Land of Round Door Knobs and Soft Toilet Paper. He had survived thousands of bullets without a scratch. He was flying in the front seat on an orientation sortie north of Dien Bien Phu with new guy Tom Shera in the back seat when a Golden BB ripped into the airplane and hit Siegwalt in the right arm and chest. Siegwalt collapsed, pulling the stick back into his lap. The aircraft started a sharp climb headed for a stall and a rendezvous with the Reaper.

Shera scrambled to finish installing an auxiliary stick in the rear so he could fly the plane. He pushed over to prevent a stall and flew back to home base at Luang Prabang, Laos. An Air America (CIA) C-123 *Provider* was waiting on the ramp to carry Siegwalt to a hospital at Udorn Royal Thai Air Force Base, Thailand. By the time the *Provider* arrived, Siegwalt was dead, a victim of a Golden BB only days before his dangerous tour was to end.

Siegwalt was replaced by Charles "Bing" Ballou, who came out of the starting gate like a thoroughbred itching for action. On his fifth day in Laos, Ballou's *Bird Dog* got shot up. He limped for home at Long Tieng, a secret CIA base in the Laotian mountains, but his engine failed. Ballou died when his O-1 crashed as he attempted a dead stick landing on a mountain. In a week's time, the Reaper took Siegwalt at the *end* of his tour and Ballou at the *beginning* of his. The Golden BB was indifferent to time. So was the Reaper.

During his clandestine tour with the *Ravens*, Sam Deichelman, son of a general, wore his blond hair tied in a pig tail. He routinely wore a surfer tee shirt, jeans, and sandals. Although he was gentle among the orphans of Long Tieng, he was a terror in the plane. By anyone's standards, he took a lot of risks. He had flown C-130 *Blindbat* gunship missions at night over the Ho Chi Minh Trail before volunteering to be a *Raven*, so he knew Laos well. As a *Blindbat* pilot he had never taken a hit, even though he often had flown through skies full of flak and hail storms of small arms fire. Flying as a *Raven* exposed him to even greater dangers.

While was flying near the Plain of Jars, a Golden BB tore through the skin of the plane and barely missed him before lodging in the chest of his back seat observer, a Laotian named Vong Chou. As quickly as possible, Deichelman flew

Chou to a hospital where quick action by medics saved his life.

Deichelman's flying became even more aggressive. He regularly took massive risks and came through unscathed. His boss sent him on a decompression trip to Bien Hoa, Vietnam to pick up a brand new *Bird Dog*. On the return trip to Laos, Deichelman was lost and never found. The Reaper never took a day off.

Deichelman was replaced at Long Tieng by Ron "Papa Fox" Rinehart, who was a glutton for combat flying. He logged over 280 combat flying hours in a single month. He often tempted the Reaper by engaging the enemy for so long that his fuel quantity needle flirted with "zero." In one close escape from the Reaper, Rinehart's engine quit for lack of fuel just as he touched down on landing at Long Tieng. On another mission, a bullet slammed through the floor of his plane and barely missed his face. Another Golden BB hit his engine and froze it. He made an emergency landing near the Chinese border, and, after hours of evading North Vietnamese ground troops, he was rescued by an Air America helicopter pilot.

Rinehart frustrated the Reaper mightily on a miserable, wet day when jet fighter planes were grounded for weather. Rinehart made several roundtrips in his *Bird Dog* to load up on rockets, high explosives, and hand grenades which he proceeded to drop out of an open window onto the enemy. His unconventional attacks not only drove back a force of North Vietnamese trying to overrun an outpost near Na Khang, they left the Reaper empty-handed.

Hank Allen flew 400 combat missions during his tour. He was scheduled to return to the States to marry his fiancée in two weeks. His last flight in Laos was a combination of an orientation hop and a check ride for newcomer Dick Ezinga. After takeoff from Vientiane, Allen reported airborne to *Cricket*, the daytime airborne command post, and that was it. The Grim Reaper snuffed out the lives of both pilots, and search and rescue attempts never uncovered a trace of either the pilots or their airplane.

Texan Fred "Cowboy" Platt was considered colorful even by *Raven* standards. He crashed or was shot down a total of 11 times. He had a soft spot for women and children, expressed, of course, in different ways. When he received the gift of a Himalayan black bear cub from Laotian kids, he fed it and trained it as lovingly as any doting father. He took the bear flying occasionally. He joked that the bear cub liked combat flying better than some of the Laotian back-seaters. When the bear wandered away and was killed by a pack of dogs, the children consoled Platt by bringing him a tiger cub with a nasty disposition. Platt's attempts to civilize the tiger usually ended badly. Repeated maulings left Platt looking as though he had arm-wrestled a chain saw.

Platt was known as a man of action. For example, he was piloting a U-17 *Skywagon* with a Laotian observer seated beside him when a 14.5 millimeter anti-aircraft round of the Golden BB variety shattered one of the Laotian's legs. Flying with his feet, Platt restrained the thrashing Laotian to apply a tourniquet, but the loss of blood was alarming. Platt knew the man would bleed out before reaching the nearest base, so, he held the Laotian with one hand and, wielding a Bowie knife with the other, amputated the Laotian's ruined leg. He applied a tourniquet that stemmed the flow of blood and flew the wounded man to Xam Thong, Laos. Platt flew back to control a flight of F-105 *Thuds*. The Laotian amputee lived.

On one awful, overcast day when a flight of *Phantoms* couldn't get through the storm clouds to hit a petroleum storage area east of Xieng Khouang, Laos, Platt took matters into his own hands. Impervious to the danger, he rolled his

Bird Dog into a dive to fire rockets at the target. Platt's first-time back-seater was a slender Laotian infantry lieutenant whose interest in aviation was on the wane because of a stream of green 12.7 millimeter anti-aircraft gun tracers racing by the cockpit. Platt destroyed the fuel dump, but, either by skill or luck, a North Vietnamese gunner put Platt's engine out of commission. Platt crash landed on a camouflaged road. Platt's harness snapped on impact and he was slammed into the instrument panel, smashing his nose and injuring both legs. The propeller dug into a berm and the airplane flipped onto its back. Platt quickly collected his map case, an M-79 grenade launcher, a bandolier of shells, a Swedish-K submachine gun, and a bag of ammo. The Laotian back-seater was frozen in fear, so Platt threw him over his shoulder and sprinted for cover.

Dave Ankerberg, an Air America HH-34 *Choctaw* helicopter pilot, responded to the call for rescue. After Ankerberg had descended low enough over Platt's hiding place, Platt boosted the Laotian back-seater into the *Choctaw* and then dove in himself. Arriving at Long Tieng, Platt headed for a T-28 *Trojan*, dragging his reluctant Laotian back-seater with him. Platt told armorers to load the *Trojan* with bombs and rockets so he could go back and retrieve the guns and ammo he had left behind.

The Laotian back-seater was last seen wandering off to un-volunteer for flight duty so he could return to his former career as a ground soldier. A doctor arrived on the scene in time to nix Platt's plan to fly. The doctor diagnosed Platt as being in a state of shock. Platt consoled himself by a night of drinking with his fellow *Ravens*. When he awoke the following morning, his broken nose was swollen and sore, but, to his surprise, the pain in his neck, back, and knees was gone. X-rays revealed that Platt's neck was broken and that his spine was fractured in seven places. He was paralyzed from the neck down. Death wasn't the only fate being handed out by the Grim Reaper.

The Reaper worked overtime to snag Mike Cavanaugh on a particularly bad weather day during which Cavanaugh had worked ten flights of jet fighters. Riding in Cavanaugh's back seat was Moonface, a Laotian back-seater not psychologically well-suited for the work he was doing. When Cavanaugh's fuel gauge told him he could barely make it back to Long Tieng before becoming a glider, he turned toward home, only to be informed by *Cricket* that Long Tieng was closed by fog and heavy rain. His only alternative landing field was Muong Soui, Laos. The weather was terrible there, too, and the North Vietnamese occupied the southern end of the airfield, but a fellow *Raven* radioed that a secret stash of fuel was hidden on the north end of the base. Cavanaugh called in A-1 *Sandies* from Nakhon Phanom, Thailand to bomb and strafe enemy troops so Cavanaugh could land on the other end of the strip. Moonface was so terrified by the bombing and anti-aircraft fire that he stayed glued to the back seat of the *Bird Dog* sobbing. When Cavanaugh finally got him out of the O-1, sense of smell told him that the poor fellow had defecated in his pants.

Cavanaugh found a 50-gallon drum, but he couldn't open the threaded plug of the drum. He broke off the wooden handles of his .38 pistol and used the skeletal metal frame as a slotted lever to unscrew the drum cap. He assigned Moonface the job of hand-pumping fuel into the *Bird Dog*. Cavanaugh climbed up on the wing to secure the hose nozzle. Bombs and rockets were exploding a couple of thousand feet away and rain was pouring down, but nothing could stop Moonface's hands from making a blur as he pumped the fuel in record time.

"Enough," Cavanaugh said.

"No!" Moonface shouted. "Not enough! Pump! Pump!"

Cavanaugh dragged his odiferous back-seater away from the fuel pump and pushed him into the plane. Bullets were flying all around them, and one of them hit the *Bird Dog's* battery. Although Cavanaugh got the engine started, he had no electronics of any kind. In total darkness, Cavanaugh took off in the direction he had last seen the runway while it was illuminated by an exploding bomb. Cavanaugh and Moonface got airborne.

"We die! We die!" Moonface said.

"We not die," Cavanaugh said. "We fly to Luang Prabang!"

A disadvantage of flying to Luang Prabang was that Cavanaugh had never been there before. The weather was crap. There were no runway lights. The Grim Reaper had dealt himself a pretty good hand. Luckily for Cavanaugh and Moonface, Don Moody, the commander of the local air operations center, was on duty. He heard the sound of an O-1 overhead and drove to the approach end of the runway to train his headlights on the landing zone, providing enough light for Cavanaugh to land the *Bird Dog*. It was the Reaper's last chance to get Cavanaugh and Moonface that night. Cavanaugh's courage and Moonface's inspired pumping had ripped the scythe right out of the Reaper's hands.

Chuck Engle and Craig Duehring were flying two separate *Bird Dogs* looking for targets in the same area on a busy North Vietnamese infiltration route when an AK-47 opened up on Engle. One bullet missed his head, but another slammed into his leg. Despite the intense pain and significant loss of blood, Engle managed to remain conscious. He flew the *Bird Dog* back to Long Tieng with Duehring as his escort. Engle intentionally ground-looped the aircraft. Waiting for emergency responders to pull him out of the cockpit, he picked up the stray AK-47 slug that had penetrated his leg. An Air America pilot flew him to a hospital at Udorn. Later, when his fellow *Ravens* flew in to visit him, Engle delighted in their groans of disgust when he pulled the gauze out of the bullet hole in his leg. Engle eventually finished rehabilitation and returned to flying *Raven* FAC missions wearing the bullet (his Golden BB) on a solid gold chain as a trophy celebrating his victory over the Grim Reaper.

An F-4 *Phantom* cleared by *Raven* Ron Reinhart rolled in for its dive bomb attack against a target near the Plain of Jars. The *Phantom* literally came apart just before smashing into the ground. The pilot died in the crash, but back-seater Mike Heenan ejected just before impact.

"I was sure I was going to die," Heenan remembered. The ease of accepting his pending death surprised him. He recalled sensing a warm, almost calm, feeling.

The ejection knocked Heenan unconscious. When he came to, he was hanging by his parachute harness beneath his canopy, which had enveloped a tree like a mushroom. He was bleeding profusely. His helmet had been ripped off, partially scalping him in the process. A broken tree limb had pierced one of his hands. He released his harness and fell to the ground, injuring his ankle. When he saw how much blood he had lost, he worried about attracting tigers.

Reinhart radioed for a *Jolly Green Giant* rescue helicopter to follow him through blinding smoke to the place where Heenan was in hiding. A rescue crew chief was lowered on a winch. He held Heenan with one hand and fired his M-16 with the other as they were pulled up to the helicopter. The chopper survived battle damage to deliver the badly injured F-4 WSO to the Udorn hospital. Heenan knew that he should have been killed, but he was humbly grateful that, because of a brave *Raven* FAC named Ron

Rinehart and a courageous HH-3 crew, the Reaper had to settle for only one soul instead of two.

A lot of *Raven* pilots were killed by Golden BBs, but scores of Golden BBs missed their marks, too. The randomness of it all gruesomely fascinated not only the *Ravens*, but, perhaps, even the Grim Reaper himself.

In Memoriam

Ravens Killed In Action

Robert L. Abbott
Henry L. Allen
John J. Bach, Jr.
Charles D. Ballou
Danny L. Berry
Park G. Bunker
Joseph K. Bush, Jr.
John L. Carroll
Joseph L. Chestnut
James E. Cross
Daniel R. Davis
Richard H. Defer
Samuel M. Deichelman
David A. Dreier
Richard G. Ezinga

Charles E. Engle
Richard W. Harold,
Paul V. Jackson III,
Edward E. McBride
Harold L. Mischler
Dennis E. Morgan
Joseph W. Potter
Gomer D. Reese III
James Rostermundt
Charles P. Russell
Richard E. Shubert
Marlin L. Siegwalt
George H. Tousley III
W. Grant Uhls
Truman R. Young

Churchill, Jan. *Hit My Smoke: Forward Air Controllers in Southeast Asia*. Sunflower University Press, 1997.

Conboy, Kenneth. *Shadow War: The CIA's Secret War in Laos*. Paladin Press, 2009.

Robbins, Christopher. *The Ravens: The Men Who Flew In America's Secret War In Laos*. Crown Publishers, Inc., 1987.

Photo credit: U.S. Air Force

Roger Locher

Sabetha, Kansas
Kansas State University
Colonel, United States Air Force
F-4, F-16, F-117

CHAPTER 32

BRAVERY

THE GRIM REAPER wanted Air Force Captain Roger Locher in the worst way. The Reaper tried every trick he knew to take the life of the intrepid F-4 *Phantom* Weapon Systems Officer (WSO) who was shot down over North Vietnam on May 10, 1972.

Locher was a special warrior. He flew three combat tours in Southeast Asia, during which he logged over 400 combat missions. He was assigned to the famed "Triple Nickel", the 555th Tactical Fighter Squadron, based at Udorn Royal Thai Air Force Base for his third combat tour. He was teamed up with a highly experienced fighter pilot named Major Bob Lodge.

Lodge and Locher shot down their first MiG-19 *Farmer* over Laos on the night of February 21, 1972. They destroyed another MiG on May 8, 1972 near a North Vietnamese MiG base called Yên Bái while flying on the wing of eventual fighter ace Captain Steve Ritchie (five kills) and his WSO, future ace Captain Charles DeBellevue (6 kills). Two days later marked the first day of a bombing campaign named "Operation Linebacker II." The "Triple Nickel" launched two flights of four *Phantoms* to participate in the morning strike force. Lodge and Locher shot down their third MiG just seconds before their wingman downed another enemy fighter plane. A moment later, Ritchie and DeBellevue bagged a third North Vietnamese fighter.

Lodge and Locher were a few heartbeats away from shooting down their fourth MiG when their *Phantom* was hit by the 30-millimeter cannons of a Shenyang J-6 (a Chinese knock-off of a Soviet MiG-19). Both of the *Phantom's* engines quit and the airplane stabilized in a flat spin. Flames licked at the rear of Locher's ejection seat. The canopy bubbled from the heat of the fire, making it impossible for Locher to see outside the plane. Unable to tolerate the heat of the fire any longer, Locher punched out at 8,000 feet. Lodge stayed with plane and died in the ensuing crash seconds later. No one could confirm that Locher had gotten a good chute. For a time, he was assumed to have been killed in action or missing in action, possibly captured by the North Vietnamese.

For days after Locher's ejection, American planes flying near Hanoi detected no ground signals or radio message traffic to suggest that he had survived. Locher's name didn't appear on North Vietnam's growing list of captured airmen, but that omission could have been a ploy. Locher had gone down near the sprawling outskirts of Hanoi, a city of about one million inhabitants. The chances of an American in a flight suit evading detection were almost nil.

Safely on the ground, Locher put distance between himself and his parachute which was spread out over a tree, compromising his position as surely as if it had been a neon sign. Locher's equipment included a pistol, two pints of water, a first aid kit, insect repellent, mosquito netting, and a knife. He also had a survival radio, but he didn't use it for fear of giving away his position. He had no expectation of being rescued so far north in Vietnam, so he started moving south, intending to swim across the Red River to make the arduous journey to sparsely inhabited mountains to the south. He calculated that, by moving only in twilight at dawn and dusk, he could cover the distance in six weeks.

For the first three days of his evasion, farmers beat the bushes tirelessly in an effort to find him. At one point, a young boy thrashed at bushes only 30 feet from where Locher had concealed himself. More than a week later, Locher came within five feet of being discovered by the enemy. He covered himself with leaves and debris and remained hidden from dogs and passing civilians all day. Subsequently, he was almost stepped on by a 900-pound water buffalo and nearly discovered by an inquisitive farm kid. Locher covered more than 12 miles in three weeks of disciplined evasion. He barely survived by eating berries, a few vegetables, and drinking water of questionable quality. Having lost 30 pounds, he was hungry and exhausted when he resolved to make a stand on a hill north of the Red River located only five miles from Yên Bái. It was time, he decided, to use the last of his radio's battery power.

"Any American aircraft, if you read Oyster One Bravo, come up on Guard." It was the first radio transmission Locher had dared to make in three weeks.

Flying overhead, Steve Ritchie heard Locher's plea for help. Intelligence officers were skeptical about the call. They were suspicious that Locher had been captured by the North Vietnamese and that they were using him as bait in a trap. Perhaps he wasn't even still alive, and the North Vietnamese were forcing a prisoner of war to impersonate Locher to attract rescuers so they could be ambushed by North Vietnamese guns.

The search and rescue effort on the first day of June was composed of aircraft of several types: A-1 *Sandy*, HH-53 *Super Jolly Green Giant*, F-4 *Phantom*, and F-105 *Thunderchief*. They were beaten back by heavy anti-aircraft fire, missiles, and MiGs.

Overnight, Seventh Air Force Commander General John Vogt made a controversial decision. He cancelled offensive operations against Hanoi on June 2 and put all his resources into an attempt to rescue Locher. Over 150 airplanes were dedicated to extracting Locher from North Vietnam. Not a single American was lost in the rescue. Flying combat air patrol to cover the extraction aircraft, F-4 *Phantom* pilot Major Phil Handley shot down a MiG with his Gatling gun while dog-fighting at 900 miles an hour. The shoot-down was believed to be the only supersonic gun kill in the history of aerial combat.

Despite withering anti-aircraft fire directed at Locher's rescuers, a *Jolly Green Giant* extracted him and flew him to safety at Udorn. General Vogt flew there from Saigon to welcome Locher back home. The ovation for the gutsy aviator who had held the Reaper at bay and survived behind enemy lines for 22 days, received a twenty-minute standing ovation at an emotional celebration at the Udorn Officers Club.

Locher finished his tour at Udorn with distinction and returned to the United States where he entered Air Force Undergraduate Pilot Training. He earned an assignment to F-4s, which he flew in New Mexico, Alaska, and Florida. Before retiring to Kansas, Locher flew F-16 *Fighting Falcons* and F-117 *Nighthawks*.

Roger Locher's name will always be associated with unshakeable confidence, persistence, and bravery in the face of overwhelming odds.

Buchanan, Ross. "The SAR Rescue of Roger Locher." Talking Proud, 2016.

Michel, Marshall L. *Clashes: Air Combat Over North Vietnam 1965–1972.* Naval Institute Press, 1997.

Steinman, Ron. *The Soldiers' Story: Vietnam in Their Own Words.* Barnes & Noble Publishing, 2000.

Kevin "VEGA" Llewelyn

Ammanford, Wales
University College of Wales, Swansea and
Britannia Royal Naval College, Dartmouth
Lieutenant Commander, Royal Navy
London Area Control Centre
RAF Shawbury
HMS Drake Area Radar Centre
United States Naval Air Station Oceana
Royal Naval Air Station Culdrose
HMS Illustrious
814 Naval Air Squadron
HMS Hermes

CHAPTER 33

HOME

AS OPERATIONS MANAGER at the London Area Control Centre, I came closer to experiencing the horror of witnessing a mid-air collision in the year 2000 than at any other time during my twenty-seven years in military aviation. I became thoroughly familiar with the details of the near disaster because I was tasked to head up the incident investigation. I couldn't possibly know of the intensely personal twist the story would take.

My investigation uncovered a number of errors, misunderstandings, and false assumptions. *Fist*, a flight of four military Hawker Sidley British Aerospace *Sea Harrier* fighter jets, had just completed low level training over Wales. Because of miserable weather, the *Fist* Flight Leader requested individual recoveries to his home base at a Royal Naval Air Station in Somerset, England. *Fist One* and *Fist Two* maintained visual contact with one other and joined up as an element as they climbed away from their low-level routes. Element Leader *Fist One* requested radar service from London Area Control Centre.

The London Area controller receiving the call had handled *Fist One* as a flight of four jets earlier in the day. The notion of four aircraft in a single formation was planted in his mind. He incorrectly assumed that *Fist One,* now a flight of two aircraft, was still composed of four *Sea*

Harriers. The controller assigned a four-digit transponder code to *Fist One* and improperly abbreviated the call sign to *Fist* instead of *Fist One*.

The *Sea Harrier* section leader repeated the assigned transponder code and correctly responded "*Fist One* and *Two*, Roger."

The controller diligently de-conflicted the *Sea Harriers'* proposed route of flight without knowing that his improper abbreviation of the flight as *Fist* had started a sequence of misunderstandings and assumptions leading toward catastrophe. The controller opened a landline to Air Traffic Control at the Naval Air Station to coordinate the handover process.

"Handover, *Fist*," he said.

The receiving controller found the phrase amusing. "Ha, that's a good one – hand-over-fist."

The two controllers chuckled at the unexpected idiom formed by the standard term "handover" and the abbreviated "*Fist*." Proper handover procedure had degenerated into distracting, non-standard dialogue.

The London Radar controller was still conversing frivolously on the landline in one ear when he received a radio message in his other ear.

Fist Three, a single *Sea Harrier*, transmitted his first radio call to London Radar by announcing that he was low on fuel and was requesting immediate recovery to his base.

Still distracted by the landline call, the London Radar controller assumed that *Fist Three's* low-fuel call had come from one of four fighters making up *Fist One Flight*. Believing he was repeating his clearance to *Fist One*, the controller reissued a clearance on the radio.

"*Fist*, I say again, clear direct track, descend and report Flight Level One-Zero-Zero."

Fist Three was happy to comply with the clearance intended for *Fist One*. Unfortunately, *Fist Three* was a hundred nautical miles west of *Fist One*, and this unintended clearance put him in direct conflict with a commercial airliner on the main East-West upper air route across the southern United Kingdom.

Proximity sensor alarms went off at the London Area Control Centre, indicating that Secondary Surveillance Radar had detected a violation of minimum separation (five nautical miles horizontally and one thousand feet vertically).

The controller handling *Fist One* still didn't realize that *Fist One* Flight had divided into three entities: (a) *Fist One* and *Two*, (b) *Fist Three*, and (c) *Fist Four*. The consequences of his misunderstanding had caused the proximity alarm, but he was blissfully unaware of that. He assumed that some other controller was to blame for the proximity alarm.

Meanwhile, up in the clouds, the airliner and *Fist Three* didn't have required separation. They were on collision courses, and the conflict was getting worse by the second. By the time the controller recognized his mistake, it was too late. The two blips on the radar screen representing *Fist Three* and the airliner merged. The controller fought the instantaneous impulse to vomit.

Although the two aircraft were literally in the same piece of sky, the pilots in the airliner didn't see the fighter plane, and, against all odds, the *Sea Harrier* pilot never saw the airliner. Somehow, the two aircraft missed striking one another.

The *Sea Harrier* pilot in *Fist Three*, a personal friend of mine, subsequently asked me how close he had come to smashing into the airliner. I told him that he didn't want to know.

I investigated this incident for several weeks. As part of the corrective action flowing from the board's findings, controllers' licenses were revoked. We learned a lot of lessons about the imprecision of the English language. We learned about the sinister consequences that can result from relying on faulty assumptions.

In the aftermath of the investigation, I conducted a careful reading of the report and plotted the latitudes and longitudes of specific positions reported by relevant aircraft.

One particular "lat-long" caught my attention. I plotted the exact geographical location of the point on earth below the point where the radar returns of the airliner and the *Sea Harrier* had merged. I was so startled by the coincidence that I computed the coordinates again to make sure I was right.

The exact location where the flaming wreckage of an airliner and a Royal Navy fighter jet would have impacted the ground was a place I knew intimately.

It was my mother's house.

Bill Weaver

Los Angeles, California
UCLA, United States Naval Academy
Captain, United States Air Force
T-6, T-33, F-80, F-84, F-94,
F-104, A-12, YF-12, SR-71
L-1011
Lockheed Aircraft Company

CHAPTER 34

BLACKBIRD

THIS ISN'T a joke. Two men in a Lockheed SR-71 *Blackbird* are roaring down the Palmdale, California runway. At rotation, one man asks the other a question.

"Bill, you still there?"

The other man, who happens to be the pilot, answers.

"Yeah, George. What's the matter?"

"Thank God! I thought you'd punched out!"

George, the flight test engineer, was strapped into the rear seat of the *Blackbird* with no forward visibility, so, when the bright red "PILOT EJECTED" light illuminated on his master warning panel, he understandably wondered whether he was flying solo.

The Grim Reaper had been forgiving on this early January day in 1966: the master warning light had illuminated because of a misadjusted micro-switch, not a pilot ejection. Test pilot Bill Weaver was still safely seated in the cockpit. Two weeks earlier, on a test flight with systems specialist Jim Zwayer, he hadn't been so lucky.

At Mach 3.18 and level at 78,800 feet (about 2,400 miles an hour almost 15 miles above the New Mexico desert), Weaver rolled the *Blackbird* into a right bank of 35 degrees as planned in the test flight profile. An immediate "inlet unstart" of the right engine induced additional right bank and nose pitch-up. Bill jammed the stick left and forward to the stops. Nothing happened. Weaver warned Zwayer to delay ejection until they had slowed at a lower altitude, but his words were garbled by violent *G* forces as the sleek *Blackbird* broke apart into thousands of fragments of titanium and polymer composites.

During the next few seconds, Weaver blacked out from extreme forces of gravity as the *Blackbird* disintegrated. When he regained consciousness, he was in free-fall outside of the aircraft with no idea how he had gotten there. At first, he assumed that he was dead. Because he felt reasonably good, he concluded that being dead wasn't so bad after all. He couldn't see because a layer of ice had formed over his pressure suit's face plate, but the sound of rushing air and what sounded like straps flapping in the wind confirmed that he was falling.

Against laws of probability, Weaver had survived the break-up of his aircraft in near space, but a lot of ways to die remained. His body temperature of about 98.6 degrees Fahrenheit was well above the boiling point of fluids at high altitude ambient pressure. Without pressurization of his pressure suit, Weaver's blood would have boiled instantly. A healthy human heart is a marvelous fluid pump, but it's essentially worthless as a pump of gaseous matter. Fortunately, an emergency oxygen cylinder tenuously connected to his special flying suit maintained pressure.

If the single oxygen line connecting Weaver's breathing tube to the emergency oxygen bottle had disconnected during the violent destruction of his aircraft, he would have died of oxygen starvation.

Without the protection of his pressure suit, Weaver likely would have frozen to death in temperatures of minus 70 degrees Fahrenheit. The pressurized suit acted like an escape capsule, protecting his body from intense buffeting, sub-zero temperatures, and debilitating *G* forces.

Regaining full consciousness, Weaver realized he wasn't dead. Although a layer of ice on his visor blinded him, he deduced that a small-diameter stabilizing chute had deployed to prevent his body from tumbling in the thin air of near space. He had little sense of how much time remained before his impact with the ground. Without warning, Weaver's parachute deployed at 15,000 feet above sea level. Although his visor hinge was broken, he managed to raise the frozen visor enough to see Zwayer's parachute a quarter mile away. He also spotted wreckage of his *Blackbird* burning on the ground in the distance.

He was descending toward a desolate, high plateau dotted with patches of snow and no signs of habitation. He calculated that he would land in the far northeastern corner of New Mexico abutting Colorado, Texas, and Oklahoma. His parachute landing was the smoothest he had ever made. Actually, it was the *only* parachute landing he had ever made. He fought with numb limbs and hands to collapse his blossoming parachute. As unusual as the day's events had been, he shouldn't have been surprised when he heard a voice.

"Can I help you?"

A cowboy in a Stetson was walking toward him from a helicopter. The cowboy turned out to be Albert Mitchell, Jr., the owner of a huge cattle ranch in northeastern New Mexico. From his ranch house two miles distant, Mitchell had seen Weaver's and Zwayer's chutes descending and had radioed the New Mexico Highway Patrol, the Air Force, and the nearest hospital. Mitchell checked on Weaver's condition before flying his helicopter over to Zwayer. Mitchell returned ten minutes later with word that Zwayer had died. The rancher arranged for his foreman to watch over Zwayer's body until authorities arrived on the scene.

Mitchell flew Weaver in his helicopter as fast as he could to a hospital in Tucumcari. When Weaver contacted Lockheed's flight test office at Edwards Air Force Base by phone, they couldn't believe that he had survived the high-Mach, midair destruction of the *Blackbird* and that he had suffered only bruises and whiplash.

When Weaver's flight profile was duplicated on an SR-71 flight simulator at Beale Air Force Base, California, the outcome was identical. Edwards discontinued flight tests of the *Blackbird* with center-of-gravity points aft of the normal range. Because of subsequent improvements to the Digital Automatic Flight and Inlet Control System, "inlet unstarts" became rare.

At the edge of space over New Mexico on a winter's day in 1966, Bill Weaver had escaped, in almost preternatural fashion, the clutches of the Grim Reaper.

Graham, Richard. *SR-71 Revealed: The Inside Story.* Motorbooks International, 1996.

Kendrick "Sonny" Bragg
1918 – 1999
St. Thomas, Virgin Islands
Duke University
1st Lt., United States Army Air Force
B-17 *Flying Fortress*

CHAPTER 35

MID-AIR

IN EARLY 1943 over Bizerta, Tunisia, Lt. Kendrick "Sonny" Bragg, aircraft commander of a B-17 *Flying Fortress* named the *All American*, spotted two German Messerschmitt Me-109 fighters attacking from dead 12 o'clock – right down the "snot locker." It was a routine *Luftwaffe* fighter tactic intended to minimize the firepower of the *Fortress's* eight gun stations. B-17s had shot down *Luftwaffe* fighters by the hundreds. Bragg recognized something unusual about the second Me-109, however; it wasn't firing its guns and it wasn't deviating from its collision course, either. Bragg assumed that the pilot of the converging Me-109 was incapacitated because German fighter pilots weren't big fans of the kamikaze shenanigans of their Japanese allies.

The Me-109 slashed through the B-17's empennage, almost lopping off the tail like a butcher's cleaver slicing off a ham hock. All ten airmen in Bragg's crew should have fallen to the Reaper's scythe right then, but they didn't.

Both engines on the *All American's* starboard side were disabled. All flight control cables had been severed except the one controlling the right elevator. Despite extensive hull damage, Bragg was able to keep the B-17 flying at reduced speeds by judicious use of power on Engines One and Two. The impact had knocked off the bomber's left horizontal stabilizer and left elevator. The vertical stabilizer, rudder, and right elevator were precariously connected to the fuselage by only a few stringers and aluminum fuselage panels. Against all odds, all ten of the *All American's* aircrew escaped injury.

Photo credit: United States Air Force

During the return to Algeria, several other *Fortresses* reduced airspeed and closed into a tight defensive formation to protect the *All American* from further attacks until they were out of range of German fighters. Once the *Fortresses* had reached friendly skies, the undamaged escorts flew on at normal cruising speed to Biskra Airfield so they could land and get out of the way of Bragg's pending emergency landing of the crippled aircraft.

Even though several eyewitnesses in other aircraft had serious doubts that the *All American's* airframe could hold together, Bragg's crew wasn't eager to parachute over the Sahara Desert where there was no assurance they would land in friendly hands. Bragg minimized aileron inputs and power changes. He landed at Biskra from a long straight-in approach. The tail of the aircraft made hideous noises as it scraped along the ground for want of a tail wheel, but no one was complaining.

Not a single member of *All American's* crew required medical attention, although it was rumored that they self-medicated at the bar later that evening.

The photograph of the damaged *All American* became one of the most widely recognized images from World War II. The image symbolized the high quality of American workmanship and, indirectly, the industrial might of the United States. The incident also showed how ingenuity and skill could disrupt the plans of the Grim Reaper.

Caiden, Martin. *Flying Forts*. Bantam Book, 1990.

From an interview with Ralph Burbridge, former Lieutenant and bombardier of the *All American*. "WW II's 'All American' Separating Fact and Fiction." *Warbird Digest*, June 27, 2013.

John T. Halliday

California
University of Miami
Lieutenant Colonel, United States Air Force
C-133, C-123, C-5
B-767
American Airlines

CHAPTER 36

MIG-17

THE GRIM REAPER doesn't play fair. In an aerial engagement between a MiG-17 *Fresco* armed with guns and missiles and an unarmed C-123 *Provider*, the MiG should win every time. Unless ... what if the C-123 pilot hoodwinked the hostile fighter pilot and the Grim Reaper with a series of imaginative, desperate, gutsy maneuvers?

If evading over a thousand rounds of small arms and anti-aircraft gun fire can be called routine, then Aircraft Commander First Lieutenant John Halliday and his crew were flying a routine secret night mission over the Ho Chi Minh Trail in Laos when a radio transmission cancelled "routine" for the night. The warning on Guard frequency was issued by *Arizona Pete*, an American radar station situated on Monkey Mountain, north of China Beach, not far from Da Nang, Viet Nam.

"Bandit! Bandit! Bandit! This is *Arizona Pete* on guard. Do not reply...." The controller went on to give azimuth and range information on the enemy aircraft, but the transmission was intermittent because Halliday and his crew were flying low over rough terrain at a considerable distance from Monkey Mountain.

Halliday scarcely noticed the warning at first because he was concentrating on dropping flares to protect friendly ground forces from being overrun by a numerically superior force of Viet Cong fighters. Pilots in the "Candlestick" Squadron – the 606th Special Operations Squadron flying out of Nakhon Phanom Air Base, Thailand – supported the ground forces virtually every night.

A *Candlestick* C-123 had never been attacked by a MiG, so Halliday initially regarded the bandit call as little more than an advisory. The MiG-17 was most likely on the prowl for some other American aircraft to the east over Vietnam. It was pretty common for North Vietnamese fighters to be guided by ground radar controllers to make high-speed passes on individual American planes or even formations of American airplanes to launch missiles or fire guns quickly before dashing away to the safety of their protected air fields.

As Halliday's navigator plotted the bandit positions in subsequent *Arizona Pete* calls, however, troubling evidence emerged. The MiG-17 was closing in for the kill on Halliday's *Provider* at a rate of nine miles a minute. The navigator estimated that the MiG would reach missile firing range in three minutes. Halliday radioed for fighter support from *Moonbeam,* the C-130 Air Command Center flying overhead. *Moonbeam* told him that fighter support was twenty minutes away. Halliday didn't have 20 minutes to spare. The MiG-17 was closing fast and would be in firing range in just over two minutes.

Halliday ordered his crew to close the aft cargo doors and to fire up the two jet engines located outboard of the *Provider's* reciprocating engines. Halliday's cargo plane had no radar jamming equipment. The only "high tech" device available to him on board was a gold-plated eye patch to protect the vision of one eye in the event of a nuclear detonation. A hundred golden eye patches wouldn't prevent Halliday from being blown out of the sky by the approaching MiG pilot. Halliday was certain that the MiG pilot must be drooling in anticipation by that point.

The MiG pilot had a lot of tools to kill the C-123. If able to discriminate the *Provider's* radar return from ground clutter, the MiG pilot could launch as many as four *Alkali* radar-guided missiles. Inside of radar missile parameters, the MiG pilot could fire 23-millimeter guns or a 37-millimeter cannon or both.

Halliday sarcastically inventoried his defensive tools: a starlight scope (for viewing the Ho Chi Minh Trail at night), a gold eye patch, and a janitor's broom. Halliday's loadmaster suggested deploying chaff to befuddle the MiG's radar, but Halliday vetoed the idea because it was too likely to pinpoint the *Provider's* position if the MiG hadn't yet detected it on his radar.

Halliday rolled into a descending turn toward a familiar valley for protection. He dove down below the tops of sheer karst walls that were faintly visible in the moonlight. Three miles separated the valley's craggy ridgelines. The valley ran straight at first then made a forty-five degree left turn and, narrowing, turned abruptly ninety degrees to the right.

As he flew down into the valley, Halliday was mortified to see a mass of clouds filling the valley straight ahead. Not only was he risking the lives of his crew by flying between great saw-toothed peaks at night, he was about to fly above the cloud deck where his C-123 would stand out in the moonlight like a tarantula on a Palomino.

"Two miles and closing fast!" Halliday's navigator said on the intercom.

Halliday faced almost certain death-by-missile by staying above the clouds or a likely death-by-rocks if he did the unthinkable – fly into the cloud bank. Inside the clouds, he would have to rely on his navigator to give him time and distance information and magnetic headings to steer clear of the steep valley walls. Either way, death could come quickly. Halliday later called it Russian Roulette with five of the six chambers loaded. He dove for the clouds and his navigator hacked a stop watch.

Arizona Pete issued another bandit warning on guard.

"One minute 'til merge," the navigator called.

Halliday made another unpredictable move to complicate the MiG's firing solution by slowing the C-123 from 150 knots to75 knots where he started to feel the onset of a stall like the nibble of a fish on a fishing line.

"Give me twenty-eight hundred rpm!" Halliday shouted to his engineer.

"Thirty seconds 'til the MiG fires!" the navigator said.

"Set max manifold pressure!" Halliday barked.

The engineer shoved both throttles toward the firewall. Halliday trimmed the aircraft for level flight as the speed decreased rapidly to fifty knots, well below stall speed. The *Provider* was hanging on the props, the high-camber wings flying in prop wash. The angle of attack was so great that Halliday felt like an astronaut balanced on top of an Apollo rocket on a Launchpad. Miraculously, the *Provider* didn't stall.

The MiG overshot.

The navigator's dead reckoning was complicated by the dramatic speed changes Halliday had induced, but he averaged the speeds out and called the forty-five degree turn.

"Left now!"

Halliday couldn't bank for the turn because he couldn't afford to lose the lift, so he toggled the right-jet electric switch to max, using assymetric thrust to fishtail the aircraft left to the new heading. He knew full well that the airplane would explode against the face of the karst if computations by the navigator were wrong.

Arizona Pete issued another bandit warning, making it clear that the MiG was coming back for another pass. Halliday felt like a maverick steer being herded into a box canyon. With his options apparently exhausted, Halliday decided to do the unexpected one more time. He charged directly toward the path of the MiG. He lowered the nose of the aircraft and called for maximum power on all engines. The airspeed indicator creeped up toward 180 knots.

"Thirty seconds 'til the hard right turn!" the navigator said. If his calculations were wrong, they would know in the most dramatic way possible without warning. "The MiG'll merge with us right at the turn!" The navigator shouted. Sweat. Racing pulse. Taste of adrenalin on the tongue. "Ten seconds 'til the turn."

The MiG had to be directly overhead.

"Turn right ninety degrees!"

Halliday slammed in full right rudder, toggled the right jet to idle, and pulled the yoke hard into his belly. Lots of Gs. Wings almost vertical. Halliday expected to smash into the cruel walls of the valley at any moment. The MiG overshot a second time. Too low to hear *Arizona Pete*, Halliday strained to fight the Gs when he heard *Moonbeam* relay a transmission from *Arizona Pete*.

"The Mig-17 is bugging out! You're clear of the threat, *Candlestick*!"

"Max power both jets!" Halliday called as he unloaded back pressure and rolled the wings level. "Let's get out of here!"

Feeling like a pearl diver gasping for air after being submerged too long, Halliday pointed the airplane steeply upward. The *Provider* popped out of the cloud deck smack dab in the middle of the valley! The navigator's time-and-distance calculations and map-reading had been perfect!

The MiG-17 had showed up for the hunt with every possible advantage – ground radar vectors, airspeed, thrust, turning radius, radar, and armament. But the MiG driver was up against an innovative opponent in Halliday.

In the face of certain disaster, Halliday had trusted his instincts to exploit unconventional techniques to break the Grim Reaper's back. The *Candlestick* crew had stalemated a MiG-17 on a harrowing night when a stalemate tasted exactly like a victory.

Halliday, John. *Flying Through Midnight, A Pilot's Dramatic Story of His Secret Missions Over Laos During the Vietnam War*. Scribner, 2005.

Frank Hemko

Linden, New Jersey
Montclair State College
Captain, United States Marine Corps
T-34, T-2, TA-4, C-130
CE-500, G-1, B-727, B-757, B-767
Holiday Airlines, Orion Air,
United Parcel Service

CHAPTER 37

CLOSE ENCOUNTERS

ONCE UPON A TIME, a Navy buddy of mine named Ken was flying out of Cubi Point, Philippines in an element of two A-4 *Skyhawks* on a target-towing mission. Target-towing was way down the list of duty preferences in the opinions of most pilots. The point of the exercise was for a surface ship to shoot the target with an *unarmed* anti-aircraft missile. (Nothing could go wrong here!)

Ken was minding his own business flying formation on his leader, and, like any good wingman, he occasionally scanned inside his own cockpit, checking instruments and indicators. During one such scan, Ken felt his airplane shudder. He quickly looked outside to inspect his leader's plane and then his own. His leader's jet was looking fine, but a foot of Ken's left wing tip had been whacked off by a surface ship's prematurely launched missile. If the missile had been carrying a warhead, Ken could have hung up his *G*-suit right then and there and his parents could have cashed his insurance check. As it was, he lived to tell a dandy sea story.

Thinking of Ken's near miss reminded me of some of my own run-ins with the Grim Reaper. I don't really know how many times the Reap Meister has taken a swipe at me. If I knew the answer, maybe I wouldn't sleep at night as well as

I do. What I do know is that the Grim One has taken his best shot at me at least three times.

The first encounter of a close kind happened in 1975 when I was flying a T-2 *Buckeye* down near Beeville, Texas. Over 600 T-2s were built at a North American Aviation plant in Columbus, Ohio. North American apparently felt obligated to name the T-2 a *Buckeye* in honor of the mascot of The Ohio State University, a prominent citadel of learning located there in Columbus. Brutus was the mascot's name. He bore a strong resemblance to a steroid-popping hazelnut wearing a gray beanie and was one of the creepier college mascots I could think of. Speaking of mascots, the mascot of Cleveland, Mississippi's Delta State University was a *Fighting Okra*, which raised this question: if the T-2 had been built in Cleveland, Mississippi, would North American have named their jet the T-2 *Fighting Okra*?

It seems like only moments ago I was writing about brushes with the Grim Reaper.

As I was saying, I almost got obliterated near Beeville, Texas. The Navy/Marine Corps set me up for it by their theory of aircraft separation. The Air Force used to organize aircraft training airspace by describing wedges of airspace off TACAN radials, DME arcs, and blocks of altitude. To non-flyers, it's easy: just think of pieces of pie stacked on top of and beside one another. As long as everybody stayed inside their piece of pie, no one got hurt. The Navy and Marine Corps, on the other hand, relied on the "Big Sky" theory of airspace allocation. They scheduled several airplanes into a much bigger chunk of sky, figuring that the chances of two aircraft running into each other in this large cubic chunk of air were miniscule. Non-flyers, imagine a gaggle of gnats orbiting around your head. The gnats almost never run into each other.

Anyway, I was flying formation with another T-2 on the day of my near death. Specifically, I was practicing rejoins. Visons of Blue Angels were dancing in my head. As I was closing in to rejoin on my element leader, I noticed two A-4 *Skyhawks* flash by from high left to low right. How cool. I concentrated on my rejoin. I had almost completed my rendezvous with my leader when I next saw the pair of *Skyhawks*. This time they were close. I mean really close. They were belly-up to me and so close I could have tightened the loose Dzus ® fasteners on their bellies. They flashed by my canopy like comets. I don't remember feeling emotional about it, except for a slight pre-death twinge in my jockey shorts, but I had to keep concentrating on joining lead or else I would have created my own mid-air collision. To this day, I don't know how I missed smashing into the *Skyhawks*.

The second time His Grimness had a pretty good shot at me occurred a few months later while I was flying air combat maneuvers in a TA-4 *Skyhawk*. I was so engrossed in trying to get in a position to "kill" my opponent that I had failed to keep a close eye on my fuel remaining. They used to say that a jet is a machine that converts fuel into noise. Apparently, I had made a lot of noise, because, to my immense surprise, the amber "Low Fuel" light illuminated in my cockpit. "Bingo" was a pre-determined fuel quantity at which I was obligated to discontinue what I was doing and recover to Chase Field, Naval Air Station Beeville. Well, the amber light revealed with shocking clarity that I was well below "Bingo."

After I admitted to my element leader how low my fuel quantity was, he stoically led me toward Chase Field in a climb to the optimal altitude for our gross weight, a fuel-efficient cruise, and a fuel-saving descent profile. The fuel quantity gauge was flirting with zero as we approached Chase Field.

I entertained a succession of deep thoughts like how my life would be after my court-martial and what my chances of survival were in an ejection. Historically, forty per cent of ejections caused pilot injury. Would I shear off my legs punching out of the *Skyhawk*? Would I ever sail again? Would I ever run another marathon? Oh, wait a minute, I thought, I'd never run a marathon in my life.

Roads are as straight as arrows around Beeville, which is located on the coastal plains of the Gulf of Mexico. Taking my chances by landing on a lightly-traveled South Texas road had tremendous appeal compared to the risks associated with ejection. I might even make headlines if I did a good job.

"Marine Corps Pilot Saves Aircraft!" I could see the headline in the *Corpus Christi Caller-Times*. The Marine Corps wouldn't court-martial an aviation hero, would they?

On we flew. I lowered gear and flaps at the last possible second, and my landing at Chase Field was an anti-climax. I even had enough fuel left to taxi all the way to the chocks without flaming out. What a relief it was not to perform a forced landing on a ranch road in South Texas! What a relief it was not to be blasted out of my airplane-turned-glider by a rocket! What a relief it was not to be court-martialed! What a relief it was not to be washed out of pilot training! I was relieved.

Three years later, the High Priest of Death almost nailed me near Twentynine Palms, California while I wasn't even flying an airplane! I was, however, innocently, blissfully, flying *in* an airplane as a passenger at the time.

Pilot training was just a mirage in my rear view mirror. I was flying C-130 *Hercules* night-time direct air support of combat missions eight hours at a time over the desert. Night flying wasn't the problem. Trying to get sleep between flights in the daytime was the problem.

It was so hot that my official crew rest uniform was nothing more than a pair of skivvies. My dormitory was a tent plopped on desert sand to slowly broil at 110 degrees Fahrenheit for hours. I rolled up the side flaps of the tent in search of a breeze to no discernable effect. It was like sleeping in a convective oven. I would have worn a sleep mask to block the light, but it was too hot. The runway at "29 Palms" was made of perforated steel planking called Marston Mats interlinked and laid on sand. Unfortunately, the steel-fabricated runway wasn't that far from my tent, so the roar of an A-6 *Intruder* or an F-4 *Phantom* taking off or landing made sleeping impossible. I'd gotten more sleep nodding off during televised baseball games on weekends than I'd gotten in three days in Insomnia Hell.

In a stroke of genius, our crew decided to sneak out of 29 Palms and find a hotel for a sabbatical dedicated to sound sleep. The worst hotel in Southern California would do. Anything would be better than the pizza oven we were living in. Executing our plan involved slipping onto a C-130 that was flying out of 29 Palms to a nearby airport away from the roar of jets. We could catch up on our rest in an air-conditioned room and fly back to 29 Palms before our next sortie. Our plan was motivated, of course, by our concern for flight safety and defense of the nation.

Seconds after boarding the C-130, I crashed on a red cloth bench in the back of the plane, hoping to fall asleep. After liftoff, I stirred when the aircraft rolled abruptly. I sat up and looked out a fuselage window in time to see jagged mountain tops flash by close to the aircraft. Something was terribly wrong. I knew the departure procedure by heart, and it didn't involve any airshow quality low-level fly-bys of mountain peaks. I scurried up to the cockpit to inquire within. The sheepish co-pilot admitted that they had flown the wrong departure procedure and had to change heading quickly to prevent a collision with mountain tops.

As it was, they had barely cleared a saddle between peaks. Had we been flying in instrument meteorological conditions (in clouds), we would have been splattered all over a mountain like gobs of butter on hot toast. That piece of information kept me wired for the remainder of the short flight. Skipping out to an air-conditioned hotel had seemed like a brilliant idea, but it had almost cost me my life.

I guess the point of this trilogy of memories is that the Grim Reaper doesn't care who screws up, just as long as The Ultimate Exterminator gets to collect his bodies. A pilot doesn't die necessarily because *he* screwed up; someone else's mistake can get him killed just as fast as his own, so he might as well chill out and get on with whatever he's supposed to be doing. Some people call it fatalistic. I call it realistic. Call it what you will; it's great to be alive!

Photo credit: Jan Gorzynik & Lucian Bobotan/123RF.com

Amir Nachumi

Tel Aviv, Israel
Hebrew University
Tel Aviv University
General, Israeli Air Force
Dassault M.D. 450, F-4, F-16
TIL Defense Systems, Triphase
Technologies Ltd., GlassCeraX

CHAPTER 38

ISRAELI ACE

THE GRIM REAPER was closing in fast on Amir Nachumi, one of two Israeli Air Force F-4 *Phantom II* pilots on Quick Reaction Alert (QRA) at Israel's Ofir Air Force Base in the southern tip of the Sanai Peninsula. It was October 6, 1973 and, unknown to Nachumi, 220 Egyptian fighter planes were conducting a massive surprise attack on Israel. Ofir Air Force Base was only moments away from being obliterated by an Egyptian force of 28 MiG-21 *Fishbeds* and MiG-17 *Frescoes*. Nachumi had to decide whether to follow orders by remaining on the ground to be destroyed by Egyptian bombs or to defy orders, scramble into the air, and face fourteen-to-one odds in an air battle. Statistically, either way it seemed, Nachumi had only a few moments to live.

A fighter pilot's job was to shoot down enemy aircraft without being shot down himself. A pilot could earn the title of "ace" by downing five enemy aircraft. Israeli Air Force General Amir Nachumi was destined to become one of the most famous aces of the modern jet era.

He got off to a slow start by failing to qualify as a pilot when he was drafted into the Israeli military in 1962. Undeterred, he served as an armored scout in the Israeli Army for two years. He separated from the army and began studying at Hebrew University, majoring in chemistry and physics. After the 1967 Six Day War, Nachumi applied to join the Israeli Air Force. This time he succeeded, earning his wings in 1968. After logging fifty combat missions flying Dassault M.D. 450 *Ouragans* (*Hurricanes*), he was assigned to fly Israel's top-line fighter, the F-4 *Phantom.*

Nachumi was in one of two *Phantoms* on QRA at Ofir Air Force Base near Sharm el-Sheik on the day of the Egyptian surprise attack. Nachumi's request to launch was denied. He recognized a breakdown in command-and-control when he saw it. He ignored orders, and he and his wingman scrambled into the air with only thirty seconds to spare before Egyptian bombs began raining down on Ofir.

Nachumi had escaped the Grim Reaper by less than a minute, but now he was all but alone in a fight with 28 MiGs! Once again, Nachumi defied the Reaper by shooting down four MiG-17s in the six-minute Ofira Air Battle. He and his wingman – who shot down three MiGs – sent the surviving Egyptians packing. A week later, Nachumi downed a Syrian MiG-21, and, on the next day, he bagged two more MiG-21s over Egypt. Seven kills in eight days!

Five years later, the Israeli Air Force received F-16 *Falcons* originally rerouted from Iran when the Shah was deposed. Nachumi was promoted to squadron commander at Ramat David Air Force Base in southern Israel. On June 7, 1981, he led half of a strike force of eight F-16s that successfully bombed Saddam Hussein's nuclear reactor at Osirak. Then, only a month later, he got a chance to enhance his reputation as an ace. While he was escorting Israeli A-4 *Skyhawks* over Lebanon, several Syrian MiG-21s attacked. Namuchi got the first kill that day to score history's first combat victory in an F-16. During the next three days, Namuchi shot down six more MiGs. He wasn't the only success story: during the first 72 hours of the First Lebanon War, the Israeli Air Force downed 80 enemy aircraft without losing a single Israeli plane. By the time of Namuchi's promotion to brigadier general, he had achieved 14 aerial victories and, apparently, a lifetime of amnesty from the evil intentions of the Grim Reaper.

Ahronheim, Anna. *The Israeli Air Force Ace Who Almost Didn't Make It*. Jerusalem Post, May 12, 2018.

Aloni, Schlomo. *Israeli Phantom II Aces*. Osprey Publishing, 2004.

Miller, Frederic P., Agnes F. Vandome, and John McBrewster, editors. *Amir Nachumi: Israeli Air Force*. Alphascript Publishing, 2010.

Photo courtesy of Don Rupert

Don "Sweetpea" Rupert

Shalimar, Florida
University of Florida
University of Southern California
Troy State University
Colonel, United States Air Force
F-4, AT-38, F-16

CHAPTER 39

CURSE

THE GRIM REAPER claims victims at sea, in the air, and on dry land. He doesn't care where. Most pilots experience their most harrowing escapes from death in the air, but my closest brushes with death weren't necessarily in an F-4 *Phantom* or in an F-16 *Viper*. For pure terror, few moments can compare to close calls I had while traveling the 200-mile stretch of road between İnçirlik Common Defense Installation (now an air base) and our squadron bombing range near Konya in the arid hinterlands of Turkey. The Reaper tried to bag me on that desolate piece of asphalt more than once back in the 1970s.

I wasn't traveling through the mountains and across the desert just for the idle pleasure of it. I was assigned to serve as Range Officer along with my trusty Turkish interpreter Adil Gultekin so, when my fellow fighter pilots in the 613th Tactical Fighter Squadron rolled in to drop bombs and strafe, my stalwart team of Turkish Air Force enlisted men could score their weapons delivery.

The motor pool gave me a Ford station wagon that wouldn't have met even Chevy Chase's standards. I didn't like the looks of it from the moment I laid eyes on it. Sure enough, in the middle of nowhere, a tire blew out with the sound of a howitzer shell. Adil and I replaced the ruined tire with our only spare. When the second tire exploded, we were out of Schlitz. I waited for the buzzards to circle overhead. I had seen Twenty Mule Team Borax movies about Death Valley as a kid, so I knew the drill. I tried to thumb a ride to a distant village to find a wheel with matching lug nut patterns, but I was brushed back off the roadway shoulder by a succession of lunatic truck drivers. Finally, a taxi stopped. My fear of dying in the desert morphed into a fear of dying inside a taxi as the aged taxi driver tried to impress me with his NASCAR moves.

Hours later, with borrowed spare tires in place, we were approaching the only traffic light in town when the Reaper made another pass. As I turned left at the light to drive to the hotel, the right front wheel locked up. No amount of braking or accelerating was going to keep the cursed Ford from careening through the intersection out of control. We did the impossible: we avoided colliding into anyone. I give full credit to the cat-like reflexes of the Turkish drivers who swerved out of our way. A motor pool investigation revealed that the mechanic who had installed the wheel bearings had failed to grease them. I proposed a court martial and a firing squad, but cooler heads prevailed.

The Reaper's next attempt on my life occurred three months later. As Adil and I crested a hill during a particularly twisty, mountainous part of the road, a Volkswagen bus traveling in the opposite direction was straddling the center line and aiming right at us. The bus had no driver and appeared to be unoccupied. A ghost bus! I had choices to make. If I steered right, I would demolish the Ford pickup and maim Adil and myself by smashing into a sheer rock face. If I steered left, we would launch a thousand feet into the air over a cliff, thereby totaling the Ford and killing Adil and myself. Of course, doing nothing is always an option. That option would have resulted in a head-on collision at 50 miles an hour without the benefit of crumple zones or airbags. The market values of the VW and the Ford would have plunged to zero and Adil and I would have met our maker almost instantly. I swerved to the right side of the road. With another coat of paint, we would have hit the rock face. At the last possible second, a head popped up behind the windshield of the VW bus. The bus driver had the largest eyes I'd ever seen. He swerved vigorously and smashed only the front left fender of the Ford, flattening our front left tire and bending its rim in the process. The driver turned out to be a Jordanian student intent on blaming me for the accident. Adil argued with him in French. I pitched in with the phrase, *"Bon chance!"* I think that means, "Fat chance, sucker!" Once again, I had foiled the Reaper.

I wasn't even safe from the Reaper's fury once I got to the range tower. On one sunny afternoon, as I flawlessly performed my Range Control Officer duties, Major Ed Rasimus led a four-ship of *Phantoms* onto the range and announced that he had mail to deliver. My initial thought was, "What a kind gesture." Properly delivered, mail can be a real morale-booster. The preferred method of mail delivery in the *Phantom* was to place envelopes in the speed brake and then, flying as low and slow as possible (say 100 feet and 250 knots), open the speed brakes, allowing the mail to flutter harmlessly to earth. Ed, perhaps because he was a little late for his range time, used a different technique. He flew toward the tower at fifty feet off the deck and he was doing at least 500 knots. When he popped open the speed brakes the relative wind promptly turned my letters into confetti that peppered the windows of the range tower like a blast from a shotgun. If the mail had been BBs, they'd still be picking shrapnel out of my torso. If the mail had contained any objects larger than ping pong balls, the search party would have found nothing but shattered glass and my mutilated corpse. Ah, but the Reaper wasn't through with me.

The last of the Reaper's attempts on my life occurred as I drove a hot new crew-cab pickup truck at twilight on the stretch of desert road between Eregli and Konya with Adil and an airman as passengers. The linkage between the gas pedal and the carburetor crapped out and the truck engine shut off. After we came to a stop on the side of the road, we looked in the trunk for anything that could help. Fortunately we found a rusty pair of pliers. After careful deliberations, we devised a team solution.

Adil climbed into the back seat and the airman lay awkwardly on the front passenger seat floor while I slid behind the wheel. The procedure for acceleration was (1) I would shout, "Hit it," (2) the airman would push the linkage with the pliers, and (3) the truck would accelerate at a surprisingly fast rate. The procedure for slowing down was (1) I would shout "Okay," (2) the airman would pull the linkage with the pliers, and (3) we would coast until we needed to repeat the procedure. We didn't have what you would call a "procedure" for cruise. It was either maximum afterburner or "off." The airman tried to hold the linkage steady as the truck bucked forward and backward like a spastic rhino. He wasn't afraid, because he was on the floor and couldn't see out the window. Adil and I, however, had an exceptionally clear view, and what we witnessed at top speed terrified us. We finally said, "Enough," and we flagged down a taxi for the remainder of our ride to our Konya hotel. I think the Inçirlik Motor Pool was betting on whether we'd call. Yep, they had to retrieve yet another vehicle they'd lent to us.

Once again, our cunning and resourcefulness, along with a willingness to experiment with a new plan, had broken the Reaper's heart!

Clifford Hopewell

Dallas, Texas
Southern Methodist University
Lieutenant Colonel, United States Air Force
B-17 *Flying Fortress*

CHAPTER 40

PARACHUTE

FIFTY MILLION SOULS fell to the scythe of the Reaper during World War II in a spasm of violence unmatched in history. Crewmembers of 8,314 destroyed American heavy bombers suffered among the highest casualty rates of all combatants. In Europe alone, the United States Army Air Force (USAAF) lost 4,754 B-17 *Flying Fortresses*. Only one in four B-17 crewmembers survived to complete the 25 missions required before being reassigned; however, B-17s were hardly sitting ducks. They carried 13 heavy machine guns positioned at eight gun stations manned by five dedicated gunners and three secondary duty gunners. One German fighter pilot likened engaging a B-17 formation to grabbing hold of a flaming porcupine.

According to the USAAF plan for Europe, 1,700 heavy bombers were to be assigned to the Eighth Air Force's 24 heavy bomber groups, each consisting of 72 bombers divided evenly among three squadrons. German anti-aircraft fire and fighter aircraft took their toll on huge formations of bombers, sometimes exceeding 1,000 in number. For example, the 94th Bomb Group (BG) stationed at Bury St. Edmonds, England lost 153 B-17s during 324 missions. Clark Gable's 91st BG (based at Bassingbourne, England) lost 197. The story of Second Lieutenant Clifford Hopewell, a young 94th BG navigator from Dallas, Texas, illustrates the Reaper's caprice in the skies over Germany.

On May 21, 1943, Clifford's crew on a B-17 named *In Der Fuhrer's Face* was assigned to fly at the lowest altitude as the last B-17 in the last squadron in the last group against heavily-defended Emden, Germany. One of Clifford's B-17 gunner friends had been killed by a German bullet to the chest on a previous raid. A chest-mounted parachute might have stopped the deadly round. Clifford was so sure that his plane would be shot up like Swiss cheese that he borrowed a chest-mounted parachute to replace his seat-mounted chute.

A crewmember without a chute didn't stand a chance of surviving if his airplane went down, but parachutes were cumbersome, so gunner crews didn't strap them on until approaching hostile skies. As the massive B-17 formation turned toward Emden, Clifford delayed donning his chute as long as possible. Then, a second after he strapped his chute on, all hell broke loose.

A swarm of German Focke-Wulf Fw 190 fighters attacked *In Der Fuhrer's Face* head-on and then converted to stern attacks. An Fw190 flying parallel to Clifford's plane relayed altitude information to German aircraft overhead. The Germans set their bomb fuses based on the time to fall from their altitude to the flight level of the American bombers. While firing his .50 caliber guns at attacking *Fockers*, bombs rained down from German planes above. The bombs passed so close that Clifford felt as though he could reach out and swat them. Threats from German fighters and anti-aircraft fire continued for forty-five minutes. When the Plexiglas nose of the B-17 was shattered by enemy fire, Clifford's bombardier was hit in the chest slightly below his parachute. Clifford treated his friend's gaping wound and prepared to replace him as bombardier.

Engine number three erupted in flames. Shortly after that, flak hit the cockpit and the B-17 exploded, throwing Clifford free of the wreckage. At one moment he had been fighting for his life inside a burning *Fort* riddled with bullets and flak fragments. At the next moment, he was outside the aircraft in a relatively quiet solitary fall toward earth, some four miles below him. His parachute deployed prematurely, ripping a huge gash in one of the panels.

Disoriented and painfully cold, Clifford descended through air temperatures thirty degrees below freezing. Lack of oxygen left him intermittently unconscious. He hit the ground like a bag of coal and was dragged across the ground by his chute until he released the fasteners. A German soldier captured him at gun point. Civilian looters stole candy from Clifford's pockets and attempted to steal the gold-colored bars on his uniform, but Clifford resisted. When a Dutch nurse arrived, she told him that his leg was broken. For the next two years, Clifford faced many hardships in German prisoner camps, but, because he had donned a parachute at the last possible second, Clifford Hopewell had escaped the grasp of the Reaper.

Hopewell, Clifford. *Combine 13*. Merrimore Press, 1990.

Clifford Hopewell (1914 – 2004) published four books: *Sam Houston: Man of Destiny*, *James Bowie: Texas Fighting Man*, *Remember Goliad: Their Silent Tents*, and *Combine 13*.

Ed Rasimus

Chicago, Illinois
Dallas, Texas
Illinois Institute of Technology
Auburn University
Troy University
Major, United States Air Force
F-105, F-4, AT-38

CHAPTER 41

COUNTER

THE PRINCE OF DOOM reaped a bountiful harvest among F-105 *Thunderchief* pilots flying missions over North Vietnam. *Thunderchiefs* were referred to as *Thuds*, usually affectionately. A *Thud* pilot flying out of Korat, Thailand, was required to complete 100 missions over North Vietnam to qualify for rotation back to the United States. About half of *Thud* pilots were killed or captured before they completed 100 missions.

One way to hasten a pilot's DEROS (date estimated return from overseas) was to participate in a search-and-rescue effort that required flying from North Vietnam back to South Vietnam (for aerial refueling for example) and then back North to assist in rescue operations. In such a case, a single mission would count as two of the required 100 missions. Even though rescue missions over the North were dangerous, a few pilots became adept at volunteering on a moment's notice to bag as many "double-counters" as possible. Major Ken Frank was one of the most eager volunteers of all. He was so eager to get his "counters" that the sound of an emergency beeper transmitting on Guard or a call on Guard that sounded remotely like "Mayday!" was all it took for him to spring into action. Frank would immediately volunteer to escort a rescue helicopter, fly protective cover during the rescue, or attack ground forces threatening the downed pilot. Frank's eagerness led to embarrassment one day when, in his haste, he failed to recognize his own wingman's voice on the radio.

"Mayday! Mayday! Mayday!" The transmission on Guard was loud and clear. It was so loud and so clear that it could have come from Spider, Frank's wingman. "*Pistol Two's* got a fire light," the distress call continued. "I'm heading feet wet just north of Dong Hoi!"

Frank quickly switched to Guard frequency and radioed, "Roger, *Pistol Two*. I've got a pair of *Thuds* nearby and we're on our way."

Frank switched frequencies to *Cricket*, an airborne command post to volunteer to help out. The moment he spoke his call sign, "*Pistol One*," he realized his oversight. He hadn't looked out of his canopy for his wingman until that moment. No joy. *Pistol Two* had skipped telling his leader about his engine fire on tactical frequency and, instead, had gone directly to Guard to notify the world. Small wonder his distress call had been so clear. Frank regained his footing quickly. "*Pistol One*," Frank said to *Cricket*, "my wingman has declared an emergency. I'm requesting rescue five miles off the coast of Dong Hoi."

Pistol Two's stoicism gave way to urgency when he felt an explosion on the frame of his *Thud*. He radioed that he was punching out. As Frank turned back toward Dong Hoi, he spotted Spider on his way toward the sea under a full parachute and already transmitting on his emergency radio.

King One-Six, an SA-16 *Albatross* seaplane that happened to be in the area, radioed his position to Spider.

Spider radioed, "Roger, *King*. Got a tally. Check your right two o'clock, slightly high. Guy in a chute."

King One-Six spotted Spider and set up a corkscrew orbit to follow Spider all the way down. The *Albatross* set down on the waves just before Spider did, and the rescue amphibious aircraft taxied directly toward him to conduct the quickest pilot rescue of the war.

In little more than an hour, Spider was in the Da Nang Officers Club buying drinks for the *Albatross* crew. As for Frank, he recovered to Korat safely without getting his extra "counter." What he got instead was unrelenting kidding for failing to notice his wingman's absence or Spider's voice on the radio.

Embarrassment was a small price to pay for a chance to jilt the Reaper.

Rasimus, Ed. *When Thunder Rolled*. Ballantine Books, 2003.

Photo courtesy of S. L. Smith

Steven Lane Smith

San Antonio, Texas
University of Missouri
Captain, United States Air Force
AT-33, F-4
DC-9, B-737, B-727, BAe-146, DC-8
Air Florida
Emery Worldwide
Presidential Airways
United Parcel Service

CHAPTER 42

KAMIKAZE

WHILE A STUDENT fighter pilot, I invented a new way to die on a moonless night back in 1973 as I pickled BDU-33s with savage inaccuracy from my F-4E *Phantom* on the Avon Park Bombing Range southeast of MacDill Air Force Base, Florida. Captain Ross Detwiler was the unlucky instructor pilot assigned to fly in my back seat that night.

Always at the leading edge of innovation, I had adopted a technique to access my cockpit utility light quickly while night flying by running the coiled wire underneath my lap belt, dimming the red filter intensity, aiming the red light toward my body, and tucking the light under my crotch to block light until it was needed. (The hooded utility light also made a dandy crotch warmer.)

I was *Blue Four* in a four-ship rectangular bombing pattern. A fifth F-4 was dropping flares in pairs to quasi-illuminate the target. From about eight thousand feet above target elevation, I rolled inverted on base to pull the nose down to the final attack heading in a thirty-degree dive with the speed set at 450 knots. The bright phosphorous flares played tricks on my senses, and I ducked from my own shadow on the way down "the chute." Release altitude was about four thousand feet above the target pylon, a wooden affair that was probably the safest spot in the State of Florida, considering the quality of my weapons delivery.

Ross called "Pickle," and I pressed the pickle button to release a single bomb. I pulled back on the stick, but the stick wouldn't budge. I pulled really hard. Nothing. I couldn't defecate in fear, because my sphincter was clamped shut tighter than the vault door at Fort Knox.

"Stick's jammed." I squealed like a soprano.

In a deeper, saner voice, Ross said, "I got it."

I felt him pull once on the stick then jiggle the stick left, right, and (alarmingly) forward. What little I could see of the ground was coming up fast, exceptionally fast. My mind raced among a maze of topics, one of which was ejecting. Before I acted on that impulse, however, Ross rolled inverted and shoved the stick forward until the negative *G*'s exceed the threshold of agony. The pains in my brain were worse than a college hangover, possibly worse than a stroke, which I miraculously avoided. I don't know how close we came to making a new sink hole in Central Florida, because it's hard to read an altimeter when your eyes are engorged with blood. With the nose aimed back at the stars, Ross rolled back upside-up and stirred the stick around to confirm that it was no longer obstructed.

"*Four's* off," he said coolly on the radio. To me he said, "Check whether you've got normal stick travel, then figure out why the stick was binding."

I reached for my groin to grasp the utility light. My groin was still there, although smaller than before, but the utility light wasn't. I located the utility light hanging by its coiled wire behind the stick.

"Sixty feet at six, *Four*," said the Range Officer, who was a lot more focused than I was about where my bomb had impacted the Sunshine State.

"*Four*," I squeaked in a feeble, mid-pubertal yodel.

I turned left to crosswind in a climb to pattern altitude and explained how I had placed the utility light beneath Big

Jim and the Twins. I reckoned that the light had dislodged and jammed between the stick and the ejection seat.

"Stow it." Sound advice from the man who had saved us with quick thinking and four-point-two negative G's.

Later, in the squadron bar, Ross asked, "Who's buying?"

"I am," I said. And I would gladly buy another round today for the unflappable fighter jock who saved me from myself and the Grim Reaper.

As a side note, I have positioned a variety of objects near my crotch since 1973, but never, not once, a utility light from an F-4E

Robin Olds

Hampton, Virginia
U.S. Military Academy
Brigadier General
United States Air Force
P-38, P-51, P-80, *Meteor*,
F-86, F-101, F-4
17 Victories

Steve Ritchie

Reidsville, North Carolina
U.S. Air Force Academy
Brigadier General
United States Air Force
F-4, F-104
5 Victories

CHAPTER 43

PROXIES

A FIGHTER PILOT enters into a tenuous, contradictory bargain with the Grim Reaper during combat. On one hand, he's the Reaper's proxy wingman, snuffing out the lives of enemy pilots. On the other hand, he can become the Reaper's victim in the blink of an eye. A few of the most successful of the Reaper's proxy wingmen scored scads of aerial kills while frustrating His Grimness by surviving dog fights unscathed. Others were not so fortunate; they tasted dog fighting glory but eventually paid the ultimate price.

Fighter aces comprise an elite society. Five victories in aerial combat is the cost of admission. Fewer than five percent of all World War II fighter pilots scored 40% of the shoot-downs. Fighter aces were self-confident and often flamboyant as suggested by some of their nicknames. "Bud" and "Buck" were common, but there were unique monikers, too. The following list of World War II aces with classic nicknames downed a total of 104 enemy planes:

- "Killer" – William Kane/McGregor, Texas
- "Kit" -- Leonard Carson/Falls City, Nebraska
- "Rat-Top" -- Fred Christensen/Massachusetts
- "Red Dog" -- Louis Norley/Conrad, Montana
- "Spike" – William Momyer/Muskogee, Oklahoma
- "Tex" -- John Barrick/Odessa, Texas

- "Tex" -- David Lee Hill/San Antonio, Texas
- "Tex" – Merriwell Vineyard/Whitewright, Texas
- "Tiger" -- John Tilley/San Francisco, California
- "Wildcat" -- Lance Wade/Reklaw, Texas

Great Britain's Royal Air Force (RAF) aces had their share of imaginative nicknames, too. Among them were "Cyclops" Bennions, "Timber" Woods, "Sawn-Off Lockie" Lock, "Ras" Berry, "Paddy" Shade, "Paddy" Green, and, perhaps most inscrutable of all, *"Imshi"* Mason. (*"Imshi"* in Arabic means "kindly remove yourself from my presence" or "get outta here!")

"Screwball" Beurling and "Moose" Fumerton were leading Canadian aces. "Ape" Cullen was an ace from Australia, and "Hawkeye" Wells, who logged 12 kills flying with the RAF, originally hailed from New Zealand.

"Killer" was a nickname with a variety of connotations. The press used "Killer" in a mildly a pejorative sense when writing about Australian ace Clive Robertson "Killer" Caldwell. Scotsman Archibald Ashmore McKellar's fellow RAF fighter pilots called him "Killer" out of admiration and fraternal affection.

"Killy" was a phonetic cousin to "Killer." Irishman John "Killy" Kilmartin bagged 12 enemy airplanes flying Hawker *Hurricanes*, *Typhoons*, and P-47 *Thunderbolts*.

Some World War II Allied aces secured their places in history by achieving singular feats.

John Cunningham earned fame as the RAF's leading night fighter ace with 20 kills.

The top scoring American flying for the RAF was the pride of Reklaw, Texas, "Wildcat" Wade, with 22 kills.

Jean-Francois Demozay, who was a French airline pilot before the war, joined the *L'Armée de l'Air* in 1939. At the end of the French campaign he found a damaged *Bombay* transport airplane on the airfield at Nantes. He made makeshift repairs and flew the *Bombay* to England carrying 16 British soldiers with him. He joined the free French and trained to fly fighters. He apparently learned his lessons well, because he shot down 18 German aircraft.

Norwegian ace Svein Heglund scored 14 kills.

Rhodesian John A. Plagis tallied 14 kills.

Polish ace Stanislaw Skalski was credited with 21 kills.

Canadian "Moose" Fumerton, who recorded 14 kills flying Bristol *Beaufighters* and de Havilland *Mosquitos*, was the leading Canadian night fighter ace.

It was difficult enough to shoot down a single adversary, but the following arbitrarily-chosen World War II Allied aces distinguished themselves by downing multiple enemy aircraft during a single sortie.

September 27, 1940: South African fighter pilot Al Lewis achieved six of his 18 victories during a single day.

October 27, 1942: "Swede" Vejtasa, an F4F *Wildcat* pilot in the United States Navy, exceeded Lewis's record by scoring seven kills in a day of fierce air-to-air action.

July 15, 1943: An RAF ace with 11 kills to his credit, "Paddy" Green piloted his *Beaufighter* to victories over four German Junkers Ju 88s during one sortie.

July 7, 1944: American Fred "Rat-Top" Christensen, with 21 kills in all, was flying a P-47 *Thunderbolt* when he shot down six planes that day.

January 14, 1945: Normally, P-51 pilot Leonard "Kit" Carson's chief concerns while flying combat were (1) freezing to death after ditching in the English Channel, (2) being tortured to death after being taken prisoner, and (3) being "massacred" by a mob of angry German civilians, which he considered likely if he hung around a "a wrecked P-51 *Mustang* with 19 swastikas painted on its side." That's why he carried two extra clips of ammunition for his pistol.

As his flight of P-51s and the bombers they were escorting approached Berlin, Carson was burdened by another worry: the urine in his plastic funnel and relief tube had frozen and he needed to relieve himself just as it was time to fight. This kind of pressure, apparently, put him in a foul mood.

He attacked a massive formation of German fighters that outnumbered the American *Mustangs* by a two-to-one ratio. The *Mustangs* lost three of their own, but they shot down more than 57 German fighters, a 19:1 kill ratio. Carson added five Messerschmitt Me-109s to his total victory count of 18.5. Beware of aces with distended bladders!

By the nature of dog fights, the Reaper swung his fearsome scythe in spasms of evil intent. A great many aces fell prey to the Reaper's wrath in violent deaths that ended their strings of victories. They're remembered in the following chapter, "Fallen Aces."

Photo credits: Blue Angels by Daniel
Alvarez/123RF.com & Navy Pilot
by Stephan Stockinger/123RF.com

CHAPTER 44

FALLEN ACES

LONGEVITY was a rarity for most aces in the Great World Wars. Combat life spans of new pilots arriving in France to battle the Germans in World War I averaged only six weeks.

George Thomson was born in Burma and educated in Scotland. He joined the Royal Flying Corps in 1916 and promptly crashed an airplane. He carried facial scars from that accident to his death. While flying Sopwith *Pups* and *Camels* in France, he recorded 15 *Luftstreitkräfte* kills. He returned to England where the press covered details of his career up to his pending twenty-first birthday, including his death when his *Camel* blew up 600 feet in the air on departure from Port Meadow near Oxford.

Fighter pilots often transported flamboyance to the boundaries of eccentricity. For example, Christopher Magee, a member of the United States Marine Corps' World War II "Black Sheep Squadron," was partial to wearing a bathing suit, bowling shoes, and a bandana as his *deguisement de la guerre* during combat sorties. Although Magee's ensemble may have scored high marks for comfort flying *Corsairs* in the South Pacific, he would have found it severely wanting in the event of a cockpit fire.

A more conventional dresser, Brendan "Paddy" Fergus Finucane from Rathmines, County Dublin, Ireland, was a rare character in his own right. He shot down 30.5 German aircraft during his brief career as a fighter pilot in the RAF. He likely would have scored several more aerial kills, but, after a night of drinking at the Greyhound Pub in Croydon, he leaped over a parapet wall, fell 18 feet, and fractured his heel. One of the *Luftwaffe's* worst nightmares was put out of action by pints of Guinness. He was only 21 years old when he was brought down by German ground fire over France and was forced to ditch in the English Channel. His last radio transmission was, "This is it, Butch." He was never seen again.

Lance "Wildcat" Wade, an ace from Reklaw, Texas volunteered to fly Hawker *Hurricanes* and Supermarine *Spitfires* in the RAF. He was killed in action near Foggia, Italy in January, 1944 at the age of 22.

German Hans-Joachim Walter Rudolf Siegfried Marseille was acclaimed by the *Luftwaffe* as their highest-scoring ace in the Western Theater. He was credited with downing 158 allied planes, almost all of them in Africa. Openly critical of the Nazi party, Marseille once insulted Hitler by playing a decadent American ragtime melody on piano in the *Führer's* presence. On more than one occasion, Marseille dropped notes to British forces to help them locate RAF pilots he had shot down. He was a notorious womanizer, wore his hair too long, and was an unreliable wingman. He frequently dove into British formations against numerical odds as high as ten-to-one. As a result, he collected a lot of bullet holes. He crash-landed damaged Messerschmitt Me-109s six times. Marseilles bailed out of the burning cockpit of an Me-109 and died when he slammed into the vertical stabilizer, rendering him unable to deploy his parachute. He was only 22.

Eric "Sawn-Off Lockie" Lock recorded 26 kills in RAF *Spitfires*. During one 16-day stretch, he shot down 15 German airplanes. His fellow fighter pilots dubbed him

"Sawn-Off Lockie" because of his short stature. Lock was killed while strafing a ground target near Calais, France on August 3, 1941 at the age of 22.

Australian *Hurricane* pilot Nigel "Ape" Cullen, was credited with 15 kills. He earned his nickname because of his imposing figure (not, as some supposed, because of a passion for bananas). He was shot down and killed over Albania at the age of 23.

Nazi Germany exploited a decided advantage in rocketry during the latter months of World War II. Their advantage didn't equate to mastery however, and only about 20% of the 10,000 V-1 rockets launched by Germany actually hit their targets around London. Nevertheless, V-1 rockets killed about 6,000 citizens of Britain. The Allies destroyed over 4,000 V-1s during their 15-minute flights from occupied France to London. Fighter pilots downed about half of that number. *Spitfire* pilot "Paddy" Shade was in hot pursuit of a V-1 on July 31, 1944 when he collided with an RAF Hawker *Tempest* fighter and was instantly killed. He was 22.

J. E. "Jack" Frost, a South African ace with 14 aerial kills, destroyed 23 Italian airplanes on the ground during a single sortie. The destruction of 23 planes on the ground did nothing for his credits as an ace, but it did measureable harm to the Nazi war machine. Frost was shot down on March 15, 1941 behind Italian lines, and Axis infantrymen advanced to capture him. Before they could reach him, however, RAF fighter pilot Bob Kershaw landed in a nearby field, Frost leaped onto Kershaw's lap in the cockpit, and the two took off with seconds to spare. Fifteen months later, Frost was shot down and killed by a *Luftwaffe* Messerschmitt Me-109. He was 23.

America's all-time leading ace, Poplar, Wisconsin native Richard J. Bong, shot down 40 Japanese aircraft, most of them while he was flying P-38 *Lightnings*. Barry Goldwater was Bong's instructor at Luke Air Force Base gunnery school. Goldwater called Bong "the finest natural pilot I ever met." Squadron mates considered Bong to be shy on the ground, but in the air he lit up like a firecracker. Like most fighter pilots, he frequently performed aerobatics at low altitudes, sometimes at the expense of innocent civilians. He was grounded for "shining his ass" under the Golden Gate Bridge, for flying low level down Market Street in San Francisco, and for blowing the clothes off of an Oakland woman's clothesline.

In a written reprimand, Fourth Air Force Commander General George C. Kenney wrote, "If you didn't want to fly down Market Street, I wouldn't have you in my Air Force, but you are not to do it anymore!" General Kenney ordered Bong to apologize by going to the woman's house, doing her laundry, and mowing the grass while the clothes dried.

In the air he left his introversion behind and he tore around like a dervish, favoring head-on passes for most of his kills. He scored several victories in the Battle of Buna-Gona in the skies over Papua New Guinea, during which he jinked the Reaper by pulling out of a dive "two inches above the shortest tree in Buna."

General Douglas McArthur presented Bong with the Congressional Medal of Honor. Despite the pleadings of his superiors, Bong continued to fly so aggressively that General Kenney transferred Bong to the States where he was feted as a national hero. He married a Wisconsin girl and reported to Wright-Patterson Air Force Base, Ohio to test fly the Air Force's first jet fighter, the F-80 *Shooting Star*. During his eleventh flight, which occurred on the same day as the atomic bombing of Hiroshima, Bong omitted to turn on the electric fuel pump before takeoff. Just after becoming airborne, the engine flamed out and nosed into the ground. Bong lay on the runway with his semi-deployed parachute wrapped around his body. The Reaper had finally got his man -- Richard Bong, aged 24.

South African "Pat" Pattle was credited with destroying more than 50 enemy planes over Egypt and Greece. On April 19, 1941, five weeks after losing his wingman, Australian ace Nigel "Ape' Cullen, Pattle shot down six Italian and German fighters. Following his landing from a patrol sortie the next morning, Pattle staggered from his cockpit and collapsed on a couch with a high fever and other symptoms of flu. A couple of hours later, sirens announced the approach of over 100 German bombers with fighter escorts headed for Athens. Pattle threw his blankets aside and dashed out onto the flight line in a sprint to his *Hurricane*. In the thick of German strafing runs, Pattle took off through a hail of bullets to hurl himself into the fight against dozens of adversaries. Pattle was last seen slumped over in his cockpit, his engine on fire, and his *Hurricane* headed out to sea. He was classified as Killed In Action at 26 years of age.

With 31 kills, Canadian "Screwball" Beurling was not easily identified as a fighter pilot. He was a teetotaler, a non-smoker, and a non-gambler who also refrained from swearing. He refused to eat before missions based on a flimsy theory that hunger sharpened his eyesight. His only reward for these conspicuously non-fighter-pilot-like virtues was the nickname "Screwball." In the defense of Malta, he shot down 26 German planes in 27 days. Only three years after the end of World War II, "Screwball" died in an overloaded cargo plane taking off from Rome in service to the new nation of Israel. He was 26 years old.

Irishman William Joseph "Timber" Woods scored ten victories in the Mediterranean Theater. He died in a *Spitfire* over Yugoslavia at the age of 28.

Scotsman Archibald Ashmore McKellar's initial nickname was "Shrimp," a moniker earned because of his diminutive height of five feet, three inches. Along the way to scoring 22 victories in the cockpits of *Hurricanes* and *Spitfires*, McKellar's nickname was upgraded to "Killer." McKellar was credited with downing the first German plane to crash in British waters. He was 28 years of age when he was shot down and killed.

Ernest "Imshi" Mason, as loosey-goosey a character as any fighter pilot in the RAF, was the leading RAF ace in the Middle East with 15 kills. He stood out from the crowd because of his thick, non-regulation beard. His lack of patience for Palestinian beggars spawned the nickname "Imshi", (which, loosely translated, meant "scram"). He was 28 when his P-40 *Kittyhawk* was downed by a German fighter pilot during a scuffle in the skies over Egypt.

French ace Jean-Francois Demozay, whose *nom-de-guerre* was "Moses Morlaix," recorded 28 kills before dying in a flying accident in 1945 at the age of 30.

Four per cent of American F-86 *Sabre* pilots in the Korean Conflict scored 40% of 756.5 enemy kills. Moreover, of 1,000 fighter pilots who flew combat over Korea, only 355 were credited with downing one or more MiG-15 *Fagots*. Seventeen American aces in World War II were credited with kills in Korea.

It was nothing short of astounding that Joseph Christopher McConnell Jr., originally from Dover, New Hampshire, turned out to be the highest-scoring American fighter ace in the Korean Conflict and the highest-scoring American jet ace in history.

First of all, the Grim Reaper had more than enough chances to terminate McConnell during World War II while he was chalking up 60 combat missions as a B-24 *Liberator* navigator. More than 2,000 B-24s were shot down, and, for most of the war, bomber crews were sent home if they managed to complete 25 missions.

Second, only a tiny percentage of navigators were allowed to enter Air Force pilot training. McConnell was one of the few to make the transition, earning his pilot wings in 1948. A terror in MiG Alley, he achieved his 16 MiG-15 kills during a four-month span from January 14 to May 18, 1953. On April 12, 1953, as McConnell "saddled in" for his eighth MiG-15 kill, a Russian ace named Semen Fedorets fired bullets that damaged McConnell's F-86. McConnell performed a high-G barrel roll that caused Fedorets to overshoot. McConnell gunned Fedorets for his eighth kill then turned south in an attempt to reach a rendezvous at sea with Air Force Search and Rescue forces. McConnell ejected over the ocean and was picked up by an H-19 *Chickasaw* helicopter. He went right back into action, shooting down his ninth MiG the following week.

After cessation of hostilities in Korea, McConnell returned to George Air Force Base to make Apple Valley, California his permanent home. The Grim Reaper finally had his way with McConnell on August 25, 1954 while the celebrated jet ace was testing the fifth production F-86H at Edwards Air Force Base. A control malfunction caused by a missing bolt was blamed for the accident that killed him at the age of 34. Investigating officer Chuck Yeager replicated the malfunction from a much higher altitude and was only barely able to recover the aircraft.

Dave Schilling, a native of Leavenworth, Kansas and a graduate of Dartmouth College scored 22.5 kills in the European Theater flying P-47 *Thunderbolts*. After surviving dozens of air battles during World War II, he died in a car accident in 1956 at the age of 38.

Each of the accomplished aces mentioned above died well before his time; however, a few aces lived to ripe old age despite having thrust themselves into the Grim Reaper's path over-and-over in war time. They are saluted in the following chapter, "Old Aces."

Photo credit: NARA

Eddie Rickenbacker

1890-1973
Captain, United States Army Air Service
Nieuport 28
World War I -- 26 Victories
Medal of Honor

CHAPTER 45

OLD ACES

A PRECIOUS FEW World War I and II fighter aces beat overwhelming odds to survive repeated clashes with the Grim Reaper in combat. An ace living longer than the average life span for American males was almost as rare as a solar eclipse, so exceptions warrant attention.

World War I Canadian ace Billy Barker was living proof of how hard it was for an ace to beat mortality rates on a steady diet of being shot at by enemy ground fire, enemy aircraft, friendly ground fire, and, all too often, friendly aircraft. Had Barker routinely sustained injuries at the rate he did on October 17, 1918, he would never have accomplished his eventual count of 46 victories.

Barker's day started out deceptively well. While flying from France to England in a shiny new Sopwith *Snipe*, he summarily shot down a German *Rumpler* observation plane. So far, so good. Immediately after that, a *Fokker* sneaked in for a long burst of machine gun fire that wounded Barker in the right leg. Royally pissed off, Barker maneuvered to put the *Fokker* in his sights and he shot it down.

The kerfuffle attracted a host of *Fokker D VII*s and *Albatros* fighters which descended on Barker like locusts. He shot down two of them, but, in the process, he was shot in the *left* leg. Barker passed out, and his *Snipe* entered a spin. When he regained consciousness, he immediately recovered from the spin, engaged another German fighter, and shot it down. Barker's reservoir of luck, however, was nigh on empty.

Just as he pressed his attack on still another German aircraft, a hail of bullets slammed into his cockpit. One bullet shattered his left elbow. He passed out again from the pain. Barker awoke barely in time to use his one operative limb to crash land in a field. Soldiers from a Scottish unit took him to a Rouen hospital where French doctors worked to keep him alive for two weeks before he recovered sufficiently for transport back to England.

After the war, despite the lingering effects of his war-time injuries, Barker flew aerial demonstrations for a number of years. He eventually used up his Reaper Waiver Chits, however, and, 12 years after the armistice, he died after crashing in a Fairchild biplane near Ottawa. No one considered Barker's thirty-five years a ripe old age.

World War II P-51 *Mustang* pilot Louis "Red Dog" Norley's nickname was the legacy of a losing streak playing Red Dog poker in which his luck was a scarcer commodity than his luck in combat. Distinctive among his 11.33 kills was an Me-163 rocket fighter. Norley, from Conrad, Montana, continued to serve in the Air Force after the war, retiring as an Air Force Lieutenant Colonel in 1963. Four years later, he passed away in California at 46, a score of years short of the average life span of American men at the time.

Never was there an ace in more desperate need of a nickname than South African Adolph Gysbert Malan. (One master of innuendo once asked, "Is the '*G*' in 'Gysbert" hard or soft?") Malan's compassionate RAF squadron mates called him "Sailor." Fearless, aloof, and cool under fire, Malan recorded 27 kills, most of them high-deflection gun shots, figuratively thumbing his nose at the Grim Reaper.

Malan's ten rules of air combat were still being posted on American Air Force fighter squadron bulletin boards a decade later in Korea. Malan believed that a fighter pilot should never fly straight-and-level for more than 30 seconds and that he should attack quickly, punching hard with short gun bursts, and then "getting the hell out." After returning to Africa, he died at the age of 53 from complications associated with Parkinson's disease.

Royal Air Force ace Robert Tuck's career was littered by paradoxical events. For example, he was a dismal student during his early school years, but, when he volunteered for the RAF, a light bulb switched on and his performance in pilot training was so good that one wit accused him of having a brain transplant.

Because casualties were high among British fighter pilots, Tuck advanced through officer ranks in rapid fashion. He routinely attacked German formations many times the size of his own, but instead of paying the price for his aggressiveness, he scored an astonishing number of victories. In 1941 he attacked a German bomber over Wales, forcing the bomber pilot to jettison his bomb load over a field. What would seem to have been good luck, however, turned out to be a tragedy when Tuck learned that the only person killed by the randomly dropped bombs was his brother-in-law.

Paradox continued to be Tuck's middle name. For example, when Tuck strafed an anti-aircraft gun and put it out of action, another nearby gun returned the favor by knocking Tuck out of the sky. Tuck's parachute landed him right in the middle of his most recent targets, so he expected to be brutally treated by the surviving Germans. Once again, however, the outcome wasn't what he had expected.

One of Tuck's bullets had lodged in the barrel of a German 20-millimeter gun and the barrel had peeled back like a banana. This William Tell-caliber shooting amused the Germans to the point that they overlooked Tuck's recent attempt on their lives. His treatment as a prisoner of war was no worse than other Allied airmen whose links to the gunners was much more obscure. Anyone who assumed that Tuck's name would appear prominently on the *Luftwaffe* shit list because of his 30 victories over German pilots would be in error. *Luftwaffe* ace Adolph Galland saw to Tuck's safety, befriended Tuck, and honored Tuck by naming him the godfather to the German's son Andreas. Tuck died at the age of 70.

Luftwaffe ace Erich "Bubi" Hartmann, the world's all-time leader in aerial victories, downed 352 aircraft, 345 of them Russian. He was never forced to bail out, but he emergency-landed battle-damaged Messerschmitt Me-109s 14 times. After his last emergency landing, he was taken prisoner. He was harshly treated in Russian prisons for ten years, but, upon his release, he returned to post-war West Germany where he joined the newly reconstituted *Luftwaffe*. His criticism of the F-104 *Starfighter* was subsequently born out as 116 German fighter pilots lost their lives in F-104 *Starfighter* non-combat crashes. Hartmann lived to be 71 years old.

The courage of Sir Douglas Bader, an inspirational World War II RAF ace, insulated him from censure for his arrogance and belligerence. His legs were amputated after his crash in an aerobatic aircraft, but Bader persisted in his desire to return to the RAF. His wishes were fulfilled at the outbreak of the war, and Bader went on to shoot down 22 enemy aircraft. He advocated attacking Me-109s from deep six o'clock because Messerschmitt pilots were separated from a fuselage fuel tank by only a steel armored plate. "I would keep my cheeks pretty tight if I was sitting on a petrol tank," he once said.

Bader's *Spitfire* was so severely damaged by a *Luftwaffe* fighter that Bader couldn't recover from the ensuing spin. When he tried to bail out, he discovered that one of his prosthetic legs was wedged in his seat, trapping him in the cockpit. He extracted himself at the last second by deploying his parachute. The canopy of the chute popped him out of the cockpit by breaking the restraining straps of his prosthesis. The Germans allowed the RAF to air-drop a replacement leg, and they presented it to Bader in prison.

In the spirit of Bader, two other severely wounded British fighter pilots navigated their separate paths back into the cockpits of P-51 *Mustangs*. An ace with 16.5 kills, James MacLachlan returned to flight status after the amputation of his left forearm. Needless to say, several modifications had to be made to his *Mustang* to enable him to fly combat. Geoffrey Page had been burned so badly in a crash that he had suffered 15 skin grafts, primarily to his face and hands. The pair of undaunted invalids teamed up as a pair on one outing over Germany.

"Good God," Page said, "we've got only one good hand between us." Enemy pilots didn't know that, however, and MacLachlan and Page combined to shoot down four Focke-Wulf Fw 190s and two Junkers Ju 88 bombers, all in a day's work.

Meanwhile, back in prison, their inspiration, Douglas Bader, attempted so many escapes that his German captors threatened to take away his legs if he didn't settle down. Although Bader never successfully completed any of his several escape plans, he never stopped plotting. One of his more effective attempts involved tying a series of sheets together to form a rope to reach the ground from a high hospital window. When his "rope" came up short in length, Bader borrowed a sheet from a comatose fellow prisoner, enabling Bader to reach the ground.

After the war, famed *Luftwaffe* ace Adolf Galland invited Bader to speak to a convention of former German pilots. Bader prefaced his remarks by saying, "My God, I had no idea we left so many of you bastards alive." Bader, a good friend of Galland's to the end, died of a heart condition at 72.

When Gregory Boyington was five years old and living in Idaho, his step father paid five dollars for his airplane-crazy son to ride in an open cockpit airplane piloted by an oddball Texas pilot named Clyde "Upside Down" Pangborn. The kid was hooked. The boy's last name was changed from Boyington to Hallenbeck by his stepfather. The newly-styled Gregory Hallenbeck got married at a young age and promptly ran out of money. He signed up for a bonus issued by the Navy to prospective pilot candidates. Only single men were eligible, so he changed his name from Hallenbeck back to Boyington to disguise his marital status.

Boyington largely ignored his family and his own health by drinking too much most of the time. He scraped through Navy flight school near the bottom of his class. He was assigned to desk jobs which he ignored in favor of women and booze. Japanese aggression in Asia came to Boyington's recue. He was recruited to join Claire Chennault's "Flying Tigers" mercenary group. Boyington and his fellow mercenaries were manifested on a ship to Burma as "missionaries" in an attempt at secrecy. Boyington and the other high-spirited mercenary pilots ate, drank, and partied their way through the cruise, thoroughly discrediting their cover as missionaries.

Unruly, scrappy, and wily, Boyington recorded a total of 26 confirmed kills during his service with the "Flying Tigers" in China and later as the leader of the United States Marine Corps's "Black Sheep Squadron." Marine pilots in his squadron called Boyington "Pappy." He frequently employed ruses to goad Japanese fighters into the air so he could shoot them down. Probabilities finally caught up with him and his F4U *Corsair* was shot down in January 1944. He was held by the Japanese as a prisoner of war for a year and a half. Boyington was awarded the Medal of Honor. Despite dozens of dust-ups with the Grim Reaper, Boyington lived to be 75.

Sir Hugh Spencer Lisle "Cocky" Dundas, a flashy rich boy, became a World War II ace the hard way. He shot down only four enemy aircraft on his own, but he shared credit for six others, so elementary addition of fractions gave him credit for a total of seven kills. His career accelerated at a torrid pace. He was promoted to squadron leader when he was 21 years old, and, at 22, he was promoted to wing commander. He frequently flew on Douglas Bader's wing at RAF Tangmere. Fascinated by fighter tactics, Dundas is credited with devising the "Finger Four" formation, variations of which are still in use over 70 years later. His career was almost sidelined by a stint as an instructor in a training wing.

The group commander not only disapproved of Dundas's slack military bearing, he despised Dundas's pet dog. Dundas adroitly dodged his commander's wrath and finagled an assignment right back into the war as leader of the RAF's first squadron of Hawker *Typhoons*. Dundas lived to the age of 75.

Eddie Rickenbacker was America's most successful World War I fighter ace, achieving 26 aerial victories, and he was awarded the Medal of Honor 12 years after the end of World War I. Having survived more than his share of dog fights, his worst day occurred when he was a passenger on a Douglas DC-3 that crashed in 1941. He suffered a fractured skull, a shattered left elbow, a paralyzed left hand, broken ribs, a crushed hip socket, broken pelvis, severed nerves, a broken left knee, and his left eyeball was blown out of its socket. He survived the ordeal to become the head of Eastern Airlines. He died at the age of 82.

World War II RAF ace Charles "Deadstick" Dyson, who shot down seven enemy aircraft in one day, earned his nickname by making several emergency landings without power. After being shot down over Greece, Dyson lived up to his nickname, and, having dead-sticked his plane into a field, he donned the costume of a shepherd and climbed three mountain ranges, finally reaching the island of Crete where he was evacuated on the last plane out. Despite his multiplicity of brushes with the Grim Reaper, Dyson lived to the age of 83.

Another ace who lived to the age of 83 was Germany's star ace Adolph Galland. Frequently at odds with *Luftwaffe* Commander Hermann Göring and Adolph Hitler, Galland was seemingly coated in Teflon ®. Despite his spats with the German High Command, Galland continued to rise in the ranks, and his 104 aerial victories made him a folk hero among German civilians and his *Luftwaffe* subordinates.

American forces captured Galland near the end of the war and transferred him to British custody. Galland had generously feted Douglas Bader and Robert Tuck during their times as prisoners-of-war in Germany, so Tuck returned the courtesy by providing wine and cigars for Galland's comfort. Tuck's interrogation of Galland could more accurately be described as a genial conversation between aviation enthusiasts. In latter years, Tuck accepted the honor of being named godfather to Galland's son.

The chances of British World War II aviator John Wolferstan Villa being nicknamed anything other than "Pancho" were approximately nil. After recording 13 kills flying RAF *Spitfires* and *Typhoons*, he took up civilian flying after the war, living to the fully-seasoned age of 83.

Clive Robertson "Killer" Caldwell was the leading Australian ace in World War II with 28.5 kills. He doctored birth and medical records to qualify as a pilot candidate in the RAF. He zipped through flight training and, after being assigned to fly P-40 *Kittyhawks* in Egypt, Syria, and Lebanon, he tore through German formations like an ornery pit bull. Late in the war he brought his aggressive style to Australia in the cockpits of *Spitfires*.

Caldwell wasn't fond of his nickname "Killer," but the English and Australian press wouldn't have it any other way. He earned the nickname by strafing parachuting *Luftwaffe* pilots while they were drifting to the ground beneath their canopies. It was a common *Luftwaffe* practice, but not one widely practiced by Allied pilots. He defended his actions by saying it wasn't blood lust, "It was just a matter of not wanting them back to have another go at us. I never shot any who landed where they could be taken prisoner." Caldwell's fondness for controversy, commerce, and cold cash resulted in his court martial for importing cheap booze on RAF planes to sell at a premium to American forces in the Philippines. Busted to the rank of Lieutenant, Caldwell resigned from the RAF. He returned to Australia, ran several successful businesses, and died at the age of 83.

Brig. Gen. Robin Olds is one of America's best-known Air Force aces with 17 total kills in World War II and Vietnam. During his time as a cadet at the United States Military Academy, he was named to college football's All-American team. He was known for his frank criticism of questionable Air Force strategy, tactics, and weapons. During one sortie over North Vietnam, when he launched four ineffective AIM-4 *Falcon* missiles that failed to hit his MiG target, he radioed in frustration, "Two, I'm done. You shoot the son of a bitch." Olds lived to the age of 84.

Flying twin-engine *Beaufighters*, John "Cat's Eyes" Cunningham was the RAF's leading night fighter ace in World War II, achieving 20 victories. After the war, he was a test pilot for de Havilland and Hawker Siddley. The Grim Reaper took one last swipe at Cunningham in 1975 when his HS-125 ingested birds on takeoff. Four people in an auto were killed when the damaged aircraft skidded off the runway, through a perimeter fence, and onto a public highway where it collided with the automobile. Despite multiple injuries, including crushed vertebrae, Cunningham lived until he was 84.

RAF *Spitfire* pilot Ronald "Ras" Berry scored 14 kills in World War II. One of the great honors of his life was to march at the head of Winston Churchill's funeral procession. Berry reached the rank of Air Commodore and lived to be 84.

A Naval Academy graduate and F6F *Hellcat* pilot, David McCampbell became the highest-scoring ace in American Navy aviation history with 34 kills. On a single day -- October 24, 1944 -- he shot down nine Japanese aircraft and made it back to land on the *USS Langley* with no fuel in his tanks and only six bullets remaining in his guns. McCampbell, a recipient of the Medal of Honor, passed away at the age of 86.

The Grim Reaper nearly collected a Marine fighter pilot named Joe Foss several times. On his way to shooting down 26 enemy planes in the Pacific, Foss himself was shot down near Malaita Island. He struggled to free himself from the parachute and seat as his *F4F Wildcat* sank below the waves. He swallowed enough sea water to drown a whale before saving himself by inflating his Mae West flotation device. A riptide prevented him from swimming ashore, so he consigned himself to a night of submersion in hostile waters.

Then he saw the shark fins. He sprinkled chlorine powder from his survival kit to repel the sharks.

Swimming with sharks prepared him for politics. Many years after the end of the war, Foss was elected to the South Dakota House of Representatives. After serving in the State House, he was returned to active duty during the Korean Conflict. Upon his return from Korea, he was named Chief of Staff of the South Dakota Air National Guard and was promoted to the rank of Brigadier General. He was elected to Governor of the State of South Dakota in 1954, serving two terms. He was elected as the first commissioner of the American Football League and he served as the President of the National Rifle Association for 12 years. He died on the first day of 2005 at the age of 87.

The *Luftwaffe* got revenge on G. H. "Cyclops" Bennions for the 12 *Luftwaffe* airplanes he had destroyed when an Me-109 shot down the RAF ace on October 1, 1940. Because Bennions's injuries included the loss of his left eye, his fellow fighter pilots, more versed in classical literature than they were sensitive to human emotions, dubbed Bennions "Cyclops," a nickname he retained for the rest of the war. He lived to the age of 90.

RAF ace Peter Brothers achieved 16 kills during World War II dog fights. He intentionally trimmed his *Hurricane* and *Spitfire* rudders out-of-true so his plane would crab, making a firing solution more difficult for attacking *Luftwaffe* fighter pilots. He distinguished himself by wearing red socks, bagging ten German fighters in the Battle of Britain, and rising to the rank of Air Commodore. He died at the age of 91.

Fighter ace David Lee "Tex" Hill from San Antonio, Texas lived to be 92 years of age despite tempting the Grim Reaper as a "Flying Tiger" in China and as a USAAF P-51 *Mustang* fighter pilot in the Pacific. The sum of his kills was

18.25. He volunteered to serve in Claire Chennault's First American Volunteer Group flying P-40 *Warhawks* in China. Later, after returning to the USAAF, he was credited with being the first P-51 pilot to down a Japanese *Zero*. He remained in the Air Force after the war and rose to the rank of Brigadier General.

Long before American Chuck Yeager became the first man to exceed the speed of sound in level flight, he achieved his first combat kill in a P-51 *Mustang*. Soon after that victory, he was shot down over France. He escaped to Spain and, contrary to Air Force policy, returned to combat flying in the 363rd Fighter Squadron. By the end of World War II, he had recorded 11.5 kills, one of which was a jet-powered Me-262.

Yeager broke two ribs while riding horses two days before piloting the Bell X-1 to record the first supersonic flight in history. As cunning as he was courageous, he persuaded a veterinarian to tend to his broken ribs so there would be no medical records of his treatment and so he wouldn't be scratched as the pilot of the X-1 that set the speed record. On the day of the record-setting flight, Yeager was in so much pain that he used a broom handle as a lever to seal the X-1 canopy latch, but he got the job done. On Yeager's most recent birthday, he was 95.

Danish ace Kaj Birkste, who piloted a World War II RAF *Spitfire* to ten kills, lived to be 96 years old. A leading World War II ace from New Zealand, Colin F. Gray claimed 27 confirmed kills. He died at 97.

Two of America's most recent jet aces are still alive. Brigadier General Richard Stephen "Steve" Ritchie, born in 1942 and educated at the United States Air Force Academy, was the United States Air Force's only pilot ace in the Vietnam War. He shot down five MiG-21 *Fishbeds*. Commander Randy "Duke" Cunningham, born in 1941 and educated at the University of Missouri, was the United States Navy's top pilot ace in the Vietnam War with five kills.

Dog fighting evolved as the harshest, most elegant, most dramatic combat ritual in history. By surviving dozens of life-and-death battles, these old aces have debunked the time-worn trope, "Only the good die young." Their triumphs over death during clashes in the air set the Reaper to mourning and authored the Reaper's lament.

Image credit: Nomadsoul1/depositphotos.com

The Grim Reaper

CHAPTER 46

SUMMING UP

WHEN THE GRIM REAPER calls your name, it can cut three ways: (1) he can snuff out your life in an instant, (2) he can screw up and you never realize he was even there, or (3) you can be aware that he missed you by such a narrow margin that you marvel that you're still alive. This book is about the third kind of encounter – the brush with death that leaves you with a trembling hand and a grateful heart.

I'm thankful to contributors for sharing recollections of their aviation close calls with death. Although their voices are distinct and varied, they share a common characteristic: they all survived one or more close encounters with the Grim Reaper and went on to lead rich, productive lives. As attached as I am to the stories related by old friends, the recollections of aviators I've never met have made me wish I had benefitted from their friendship long ago.

As the theme of the book suggests, the Grim Reaper awaits us all. When my turn comes to head West, I hope I'll conduct myself with the grace and courage displayed by my contributors in these pages.

Books by Contributors

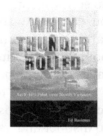

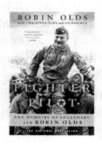
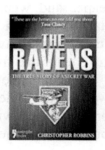

Books by Contributors

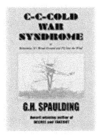
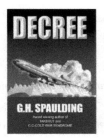

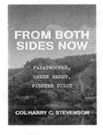
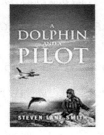
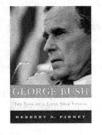

BIBLIOGRAPHY

Bergström, Christer. *The Battle of Britain: An Epic Conflict Revisited*. Casemate, 2015.

Brickhill, *Paul. Reach for the Sky: The Story of Douglas Bader DSO, DFC*. Oldhams Press, 1954.

Boyington, Gregory "Pappy." *Baa Baa Black Sheep*. Wilson Press, 1958.

Coram, Robert. *Boyd: The Fighter Pilot Who Changed the Art of War*. Little, Brown and Company, 2002.

Dorr, Robert F. *Korean War Aces*. Osprey, 1995.

Ethell, Jeffrey and Alfred Price. *One Day in a Very Long War: May 10, 1972*. Random House, 1989.

Ford, Daniel. *Flying Tigers: Claire Chennault and the American Volunteer Group*. Smithsonian History of Aviation, 1995.

Edwards, Ted. *Seven at Santa Cruz: The Life of Fighter Ace Stanley "Swede" Vejtasa*. Naval Institute Press, 2018.

Golley, John. *John "Cat's-Eyes" Cunningham: The Aviation Legend*. Airlife Publishing Ltd, 1999.

Gurney, Gene. *Five Down and Glory*. G. P. Putnam's Sons, 1958.

Hess, William N. *The American Aces of World War II and Korea*, Arco Publishing, 1968.

Holmes, Tony. *Hurricane Aces 1939 - 1940*. Osprey Publishing, 1998.

Kaplan, Philip. *Fighter Aces of the Luftwaffe in World War WWII*. Pen & Sword Aviation, 2007.

Kurowski, Franz. *German Fighter Ace: Hans-Joachim Marseille: Star of Africa.* Schiffer Military History, 1994.

Matthews, Andrew Johannes, and John Foreman. *Luftwaffe Aces — Biographies and Victory Claims.* Red Kite, 2015.

McConnell, Malcolm. *Into the Mouth of the Cat.* Signet, 1986.

Miller, Thomas G. *Cactus Air Force.* Harper and Row, 1969.

Rasimus, Ed and Christina Olds. *Fighter Pilot: The Memoirs of Legendary Ace Robin Olds.* St. Martin's Press, 2010.

Rickenbacker, Edward V. *Rickenbacker: An Autobiography.* Prentice-Hall, Inc., 1967.

Scutts, Jerry. *Mustang Aces of the Eighth Air Force.* Osprey Publishing, 1994.

Shores, Christopher, Brian Cull, and Nicola Malizia. *Air war for Yugoslavia, Greece and Crete.* Grub Street, 1987.

Smith, Robert Barr and Laurence J. Yadon. *The Greatest Air Aces Stories Ever Told.* Lyons Press, 2017.

Spick, Mike. *Allied Fighter Aces Of World War II.* Greenhill Books, 1997.

Spick, Mike. *Luftwaffe Fighter Aces.* Ivy Books, 1996.

Yenne, Bill. *Aces High: The Heroic Saga of the Two Top-Scoring American Aces of World War II.* Penguin Group, 2009.

Are you a pilot who should be dead?

If you are, and if you would like to contribute your aviation close-call story to my next anthology, please send a draft of fewer than 2,000 words by email to stevenlanesmithauthor@gmail.com. I welcome a variety of voices, backgrounds, and tones – serious or humorous. Include a black-and-white photo of you with a resolution of at least 300 dpi in jpeg format.

INDEX

311

313

314

315

316

317

318

321